THE GREATEST SWING BAND IN THE WORLD

(The Ted Heath Story)

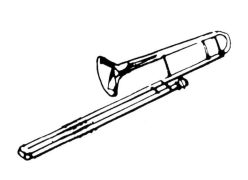

Tony Parker

Ted Heath

ISBN 0 9521782 0 6

Typesetting: LVR Typesetters, London

Design and Artwork: Tony Parker

First published and printed 1993 by
Hirst, Kidd & Rennie Ltd.
Union Street, Oldham, England

ACKNOWLEDGEMENTS

My personal and sincere thanks are extended to the following musicians, organisations and others who, unhesitatingly, assisted me in the preparation of this book, and without whose help the venture would never have been possible:—

Don and Diana Lusher; Derek Boulton; Ronnie Verrell; Stan Roderick; Kenny Baker; Tommy Whittle; Duncan Campbell; Ken Kiddier; Lita Roza; Dennis Lotis; Sheila Southern; Bob Flanigan, the leader of the Four Freshmen; Syd Lawrence; Bryan Pendleton; Harry Bence; Pete Jones, the secretary of the Ted Heath Music Appreciation Society; Derek Boulton Management Ltd; Horatio Nelson Records and Tapes; Chappell & Co Ltd; Lawrence Wright Music Co Ltd; the Musicians' Union and Equity.

My gratitude is also extended to the managements and staff of the Pavilion Gardens and the Opera House, Buxton; the Davenport Theatre, Stockport; the Royal Concert Hall, Nottingham; the Moat House Hotel, Nottingham, the Queen Elizabeth Hall, Oldham; the Grange Arts Centre, Oldham, and the Free Trade Hall, Manchester, all of whom offered me both their courtesy and facilities, and made life that much easier for me when it came to interviewing some of the contributors.

Acknowledging that some features in this book were originally utilised in part, or in articles and reviews, I want to thank the following publications for granting permission to reprint passages which first appeared under their imprints: Buxton Advertiser, Crescendo International and the Oldham Evening Chronicle.

INTRODUCTION

THERE have been numerous articles written about Ted Heath, but never has anyone spent the time Tony Parker has done to compile so many facts about the man and his music.

The Ted Heath story is a fascinating one of rags to riches. Tony Parker has had in-depth interviews with those who were close to Ted, including two of the original members of the band, Stan Roderick and Kenny Baker. Ronnie Verrell, Tommy Whittle, Ken Kiddier and many others also co-operated and assisted in the preparation of this book.

Ted used to be what was then known as a street busker, being a member of his father's brass band which played in the streets of London.

Who, at that time, was to appreciate that the young man who played the trombone outside the London Palladium would one day top the bill at that very special theatre on so many memorable occasions? Ted, as a young boy, also played outside the ground of Fulham Football Club, of whom he was a great supporter, and he finished his life sitting regularly in the director's box.

Ted's career spanned many years as a top trombone player when he was a member of the great orchestras of Ambrose, Sidney Lipton and Geraldo. His dream of having his own band became a reality in 1945, and Tony Parker details the early, hard and difficult times before that dream eventually became a reality.

Ted Heath created the greatest swing band Great Britain has ever produced and his overseas tours, particularly to America and Australia, did so much for the prestige of British music. He originally planned a sweet-music style of band, but events, thankfully, took him on another course.

Tony Parker is to be congratulated on his achievement for this long-awaited book. The Ted Heath Appreciation Society and its members, plus all the Ted Heath fans who attend the concerts of the band, which is now under the direction of Don Lusher, are most grateful to him.

DEREK BOULTON

Former Ted Heath road manager

PREFACE

THE world of the big band and its music is a mixture of all things to all people. To dancers it is a combination of good music played for pleasure in congenial surroundings, and generating the excitement and the opportunity to see a band which hitherto has only been seen on television (if you are lucky) or heard on radio or records.

The ballroom was THE place to be usually, though not always, on Saturday nights. It had an atmosphere which simply could not be manufactured, for it was one of those institutions where the buzz was generated by the patrons and complemented by the band and its music.

And no one in the big-band business knew more about creating that buzz and excitement than Ted Heath.

Some ballrooms, or palais' or dance halls as they were known depending on what part of the country you lived, were swish and on a grand scale with soft lights, intimate perimeter tables and a huge, revolving mirror ball which hung from the ceiling and cast prismatic reflections across the floor and over the heads of the dancers.

Other ballrooms, which were regarded as the poor relations, were less than opulent. They were very basic and did not possess the grand touches of mirror lighting. However, despite the differences, the one overriding factor between the two was the fact that the dancers succeeded in doing what they initially set out to achieve, and that was to enjoy themselves.

With a concert, however, it is very different, and although much of the routine for the musicians is very much the same as it is for dance dates, the occasion generates an atmosphere all of its very own. In the auditorium there is a buzz of anticipation and expectancy, and of settling down for an evening of good musical entertainment.

Here again, Ted Heath knew all there was to know about anticipation and expectancy.

So if this is what the atmosphere is like at the front of the house, try and consider what it is like backstage. Here it is a very different world, and the musicians' dressing room can be a fascinating place to be prior to curtain-up time.

It is usually a scene of organised chaos (sometimes not so organised) with musicians unpacking, assembling and tuning their instruments; of a musical director or leader finally going over the scores in a last-minute check on the musical sequence of the band's programme. Then of course there are the nerves, and most musicians have their own way of coping with them.

Not even the most experienced musician is immune to some kind of nerves — they come with the territory and are all part of being a performer. Some players will take a quick drink (if the leader allows them to do so) or form a card school, while some will probably smoke more than the odd cigarette.

There will be those who will be constantly cracking jokes in an attempt to put himself, and everyone else at ease, and there are a lot who believe that the best way to tackle nerves is by reading a book or indulging in slow, deep-breathing exercises.

It is all something of a ritual with everyone attempting to look and feel calm — a factor which the audience, as they sit chatting, waiting and manhandling their programmes, probably don't even consider with so much as a passing thought.

Behind the closed curtains the musicians take their places at their stands, with last-minute checks to see if their instruments are still in tune. It is only after the house lights have dimmed, and the leader calls for the first few strains of the band's signature tune (in this case it is "Listen To My Music") that the nerves suddenly begin to subside.

From a purely personal point of view I have been watching, listening to and writing about big bands for the best part of 35 years, and during that time I have known and met some wonderful people in connection with this very special style of music. I hope to continue to meet them.

One of those people, and the man who shaped forever my love and affection for the big bands, was the late, lamented Ted Heath. And I am sure that I am not alone when I say that Ted's band was truly the greatest swing band in the world.

When Ted died, ironically on my birthday in 1969, the world of big-band music lost one of its greatest, all-time ambassadors.

TP

FOREWORD

BY DON LUSHER

This book on Ted Heath is a must for anyone interested in the band business.

Tony Parker has done his research very well indeed and he speaks not only as a fan, but also as a professional journalist who has made it his responsibility to find out as much as possible about his subject.

You will discover many interesting facts about the man himself; his family, his musicians, the organisation, his travels, his fellow band leaders, the way his mind worked, the ups and downs and his inspiration. You will laugh and maybe even shed a tear, but I am sure you will enjoy it.

As I finished reading the book I thought: 'What a wonderful man — what a wonderful band.' And I am very lucky, and proud, to have been a part of it!

CONTENTS

CHAPTER ONE

An Introduction To a Legend

 It takes only 22 seconds to play, yet "Listen To My Music" must be the most enduring of all the signature tunes in the history of British big-band music. Instantly recognisable it can also be described as the most atmosphere-creating, and yet shortest, of openers. Think of it — hear it — and straight away it brings the name of one man to mind.

Ted Heath was a musician first and the ultimate in bandleaders second. He was the man who stamped his authority and aura on to the music scene in 1945, and whose influence to this day still remains a dominant and omnipotent force on the big-band scene more than 24 years after his death.

The name of Ted Heath had, and always will have, a magical ring about it; he was synonymous with rhythms and arrangements that encapsulated and provoked excitement, played with precision and discipline, and which above all else underscored an atmosphere of immense musical power and coupled with the utmost respect.

His was the ultimate British band which, in true swinging fashion more than 40 years ago, proved to be the cornerstone and inspiration for all the other big bands in this country at the time.

It swept all before it, conquered America, and then went on to challenge and, in the opinion of many, became better than most in the world.

That is in no way a mark of disrespect for Ted's great US counterparts of the era such as Stan Kenton, Count Basie, Woody Herman, Lionel Hampton and Duke Ellington.

True, they were all dynamic, well-established and elite bands with absolutely nothing to prove, and their names were held in awe. But the all-star Ted Heath aggregation became an institution — a musical family — which has lasted long after his death.

To have witnessed seeing him and his band in action is one thing, to have actually met him is a thing which has left an almost indelible mark. To the impressionable it was a meeting with a colossus — a legend — and one that will never be forgotten.

It was in 1953, at the age of 14, when I first met Ted Heath at the Pavilion Gardens ballroom in Buxton, Derbyshire. He was a frequent visitor to the venue and I went to see him on each of the occasions when he visited the place.

1

On one particular Saturday night while standing listening to this great band at the front of the stage (I couldn't dance then any more than I can now!) I made up my mind that when the dance was over I would do my level best to meet him.

This I did by making my way backstage and, after a furtive knock on his dressing-room door, I was ushered into the room by the man who was, in my eyes, the greatest swing legend of them all.

Smiling, he signed my autograph book, put a friendly arm around my shoulder and asked if I'd enjoyed the evening. Naturally I said that I had, and putting on a brave face I prepared to ask him the ultimate question.

"Mr Heath . . ."

"Call me Ted," he replied.

"Mr Heath . . ." To call him by his christian name seemed too familiar to such a giant of a man. Like I said I was only 14, but respectful with it! "Could I possibly meet your band?"

His, fixed friendly smile remained and his grip on my shoulder tightened. "It's my pleasure — anyone in particular?"

"Don Lusher," I stammered. "And Ronnie Verrell, and . . ."

"Come with me." said Ted, as he led the way down the corridor to another door. He knocked. "Are you all decent in there?" he called. Someone, I suspect that it was the band's humorist Johnny Hawksworth, replied: "Depends on what you call decent!"

In we went and it has to be said that every member of the band was, indeed, decent — unless you count a dozen or so musicians without their shirts, and drinking from bottles of beer, as being indecent. Which it wasn't.

Well I did meet the band, and before coming away from the dressing room a quarter of an hour later with half a book full of autographs, I was introduced to trumpeters Eddie Blair, Bert Ezzard and Bobby Pratt, bassist Johnny Hawksworth, my favourite drummer, Ronnie Verrell, who didn't even look as if he had broken into a sweat even though he had, a few minutes earlier, brought the place down with a nine-minute solo of "Skin Deep".

The final thrill of the evening was meeting my own personal, musical hero, trombonist Don Lusher. Like I said, all that took place back in 1953 and ever since I have kept in touch with Don and Ronnie, both of whom I feel honoured to list among my very best friends.

But this was the successful Ted Heath band at its height, and shortly before it reached its pinnacle of the numerous tours of the States. But what about the times before it reached the lofty position that it was now enjoying? What about the dreams and the struggles which Ted faced before he finally made it?

How, where and when did this great, British musical force emerge from a dream into a dynamic reality?

These were many of the questions which needed to be answered, and I did so desperately want to ask them that night. But, having already been treated to what can best be described as the best example of Ted's unstinting kindness and hospitality, by introducing me to his band, my nerve failed me.

After all, he was the leader of the most popular band in Britain; his famous London Palladium concerts were still a highly-popular and sell-out attraction and so, not unnaturally perhaps, my unprepared interview almost sank without trace. But not before I asked him whether he liked appearing in Buxton.

Almost without hesitation Ted replied: "I love visiting here, and places just like it. They provide my band with its bread and butter, while the Palladium gives us the jam to spread on it."

Bearing in mind that only minutes earlier I had rubbed shoulders and shaken hands with the finest bandsmen in the business, in the confines of their dressing room, it was only natural that the excitement and atmosphere of the occasion was the prime reason for my becoming overawed and almost speechless,

One thing was certain in my mind that night, however, was the intention that one day (maybe it would be a long time in the future) I would discover the answers. Needless to say that at school on the following Monday morning I was the undoubted envy of the fifth-form, when I related to the lads that not only had I met up with such a remarkable gentleman, but I had also spoken to his band as well.

You see, although the rest of my classmates, like me, had Ted firmly placed on a pedestal, bought all his records and attended those visits to Buxton, my thoughts went much, much deeper. In short, plans and ideas were already being sown in my mind for something (I wasn't quite sure what at that stage) much more interesting and constructive than merely always being an auditorium admirer.

Ted was a phenomenon and there was so much more that I wanted to know about the man and his band. And merely meeting and speaking to him and his musicians was, quite simply, not enough. All that the experience had done was to whet my appetite. I wanted the answers to those questions and I was determined to get them at some time or another.

But little did I realise that that Saturday night meeting would have such a profound effect and that later in life, when I became a journalist, it would prove to be the launching pad for this book.

Probably the best busker in the world. *(Without apologies to Carlsberg Lager!)*

Until the project got off the ground it was a case of research, questions, answers and interviews. Funnily enough the most intriguing and outstanding question was: "Did this truly great leader REALLY stand busking to the queues outside the theatres in London's West End, until he was discovered and taken on board by Jack Hylton?"

Well, from all the accounts which I have heard and been told, that's exactly what he did do.

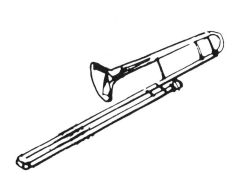

CHAPTER TWO

The Man and His Dream

TED HEATH ... bandleader and gentleman

Ted was born in Wandsworth, London, in 1900. His father was the leader of the Wandsworth Borough Band.

At the age of 10 he won a prize for playing tenor horn in a brass band concert.

He switched to trombone when he was in his early teens and, later, frequently had to play as a street musician due to lack of work.

While busking he was discovered and signed up by Jack Hylton, with whom he played until 1927. He then joined Bert Ambrose, and stayed with his band until 1935.

It was after a short spell with Bert Ambrose's orchestra (from which he was sacked) and some unstinting guidance from the gentlemanly Sidney Lipton, which helped Ted to regain his shattered confidence. He joined the ranks of Geraldo — a man who was so professional, both musically and personally, that it's open to speculation as to whether these virtues and good habits eventually rubbed off on to Ted, and influenced his own modus operandi as a bandleader later on.

Ted, at the time, thought that his job with Geraldo was THE thing. But as time continued to pass by his visionary dream for his band grew.

While playing with Geraldo, in 1942, Ted's mind was made up that after the war he wanted a band of his own. He wanted his outfit to consist of eight brass and five saxes, plus rhythm, which was really on a par with the Glenn Miller instrumentation and also that of Tommy Dorsey. Geraldo's line-up consisted of six brass and five saxes.

Geraldo used to hire the services of Max Goldberg, who was a lead trumpet player with Ambrose, and he also had players of the calibre of Chick Smith. His trombone section consisted of Ted on lead trombone, Woolf Phillips, Paul Fenhoulet and George Rowe.

Later he employed a certain Mr Don Lusher, who ended up you-know-where!

Ted's dream, for the style of his band was basically to assemble a sweet-music outfit, and not a 17-piece augmentation, featuring Canadian Paul Carpenter as a singing compere, as eventually happened.

OK, it was, in Paul's now-famous introduction, "Forty minutes right off the top, with Ted Heath and his music." It was all good publicity and it brought the band to the attention of many thousands of listeners.

Whose joke was it that amused the band — Ted's or Paul Carpenter's?

But it was also proving to be an expensive outfit. The intro was for the broadcasts which the band did during the war, for the BBC's policy in those days was to give anybody a date who could get a band of musicians together.

Ted had left Geraldo with the parting words from his employer, "You'll regret it" ringing in his ears. At first it was a great struggle to find sufficient work in those early days to maintain a band of such high quality, and several of his musicians left him to return to safer pastures.

However, there always seemed to be something just around the corner which helped to keep his band intact. And it was with no small help from Ted's wife Moira which helped to make the band financially possible. Moira, who was an excellent lyricist, wrote the words to two numbers which Ted had penned.

"That Lovely Weekend" was originally a poem written for Ted by Moira, after they had spent a weekend away. When it was turned into a song, with Ted writing the music, it proved to be an enormous hit.

Here, then, are the lyrics to that beautiful song:

> *I haven't said thanks for that lovely weekend,*
>
> *Those two days of Heaven you helped me to spend.*
>
> *The thrill of your kiss as you stepped off the train,*
>
> *The smile in your eyes was like sun after rain,*
>
> *To mark the occasion we went out to dine,*
>
> *Remember the laughter, the music, the wine,*
>
> *The drive in the taxi, when midnight had flown,*
>
> *Then breakfast next morning, just we two alone,*
>
> *You had to go, the time was so short, we both had so much to say,*
>
> *Your kit to be packed, the train to be caught, sorry I cried, but I just felt that way,*
>
> *And now you have gone dear, this letter I pen,*

*My heart travels with you 'till we meet
again,*

*Keep smiling my darling, and one day
we'll spend,*

*A lifetime as sweet as that lovely week-
end.*

———————

(Lyrics reproduced with acknowledgements to Chappell & Co Ltd)

This number, incidentally, was ultimately banned by the BBC on the
grounds that the lyrics were too risque. Eat your heart out, Madonna!

Towards the end of the war Moira wrote another lyric, to which Ted
put the music. This number, as with "That Lovely Weekend", was a big
hit — especially in the United States. More important, however, it
provided the funds to keep the band going. The lyrics below are to "I'm
Gonna Love That Guy":

*I'm gonna love that guy like he's never
been loved before,*

*I'm gonna show that guy he's the fella
that I adore,*

*When he's in my arms tonight, our
dreams will all come true,*

*Gonna hold him closely ever so tight, all
of our whole lives through,*

*I'm gonna kiss that guy like he's never
been kissed before,*

*And when I kiss that guy it'll be worth the
waiting for,*

*We'll never part again, he'll hold my
heart again, for ever and ever more,*

*I'm gonna love that guy like he's never
been loved before.*

———————

(Lyrics reproduced with acknowledgements to Lawrence Wright Music Co Ltd,
under licence to CBS Songs)

The band was now starting to strike lucky; it was doing its own one-night stands by hiring drill halls and other venues, and then along came a regular Monday-night spot at the Hammersmith Palais.

Val Parnell, the uncle of Ted's drummer, Jack, booked the band for alternate Sunday night swing sessions at the London Palladium, and in so doing created a monumental milestone in the history of the band.

Eventually the band followed this up with a three- weeks   booking at the Winter Gardens, Blackpool, for a number of consecutive seasons, which to this day has proved to be one of the most all-time remembered events that the resort has ever staged.'

Here he was fortunate for the BBC had now changed its policy and would now only give a broadcast to a bandleader who had a regular band. What that actually meant was that the BBC wanted Ted to do three jobs a week, minimum.

He made a number of records for Decca for what was a "Music While You Work" series, but he never wanted them to be released. His words upon hearing the test-pressings were: "These are no good! I don't want my band sounding like that!"

However, Decca did release them after he died, with titles which included "Caravan", "I've Got Sixpence" and "South of the Border". Ted did two or three other broadcasts a year until the end of the

The bandleader who selected a team just like a soccer boss

IN many ways Ted, when selecting his choice of personnel for the band, acted very much like the modern-day soccer manager.

He knew the players that he wanted for his line-up, and went about recruiting them. If they weren't available at the time, Ted would wait until they were free to join his team of top-liners.

This was all part and parcel of his master plan to create the best swing band this country had ever seen, and one that would be up there challenging the Stateside outfits in the top league.

Ted's determination to break their monopoly was paramount, and it proved to be the driving force behind his ambition.

As a result of his efforts he was well rewarded.

Both his foresight and energies paid dividends, for in a relatively short space of time his sound became instantly recognisable, and the names of his players and singers became household names.

The arrival of Ted's outfit on the big-band scene was to prove a watershed for the big guns of America. No longer were they to have things their own way, and the most important thing was that they knew it, too.

It was a time for them to constantly keep looking over their shoulders; Ted Heath had arrived and was now breathing hard down their necks. Their undisputed title was now very much at stake.

hostilities. After that he took on the business of running his own band properly.

In the early days after leaving Geraldo, when Ted was seeking the formula that would make his band not just a good one but the best in the land, he went about the business of the recruitment of his musicians in a manner which resembled that of some of the top soccer managers of today.

He always kept his eyes open and his ears to the ground, as he searched for new talent to replace some of the players who he thought didn't quite come up to the high standards he was seeking.

Ted was forever on the look-out for the very best men to come in and take over from some of the musicians who either left to conquer fresh fields, or who called it a day because they tired of the constant touring. After all, sleeping in a different hotel bed every night and virtually living out of a suitcase, is not everyone's cup of tea. To many it could, and was, a very demanding life indeed — despite being well paid for their efforts.

Ted's early story is based on dedication, hard work and an unceasing desire to succeed. Small wonder, then, that he expected from his musicians the self-same efforts which he had put in during what can best be described as his apprenticeship years.

It was small wonder, too, that some of those same musicians who did move on after serving under his command all paid him the highest tribute by succeeding in their own respective ventures.

But Ted knew that he was the master and so, too, did everyone else. That is why, at first, they copied both his style and methods of leadership — or attempted to — until they discovered their own forte, and how in doing so they paid him the highest compliment.

That, briefly, is the initial scenario of how Ted Heath's dream arose out of the ashes of his busking days. But what exactly were those particular days like, and what were the events which led to him eventually joining the ranks of Gerald Bright (Geraldo) and being blessed with the dream of creating the best swing and dance band that this country had ever known?

One could suppose that it all really started when Ted was 19 years old, and lived in a London where street musicians were plentiful; where bands of ex-servicemen cashed in on post-war sentiments.

The particular band of which he was a part of, and which numbered six musicians plus collectors, played regularly to the rush-hour crowds at London Bridge and choice spots in the West End including Coventry Street, Piccadilly and the outside of the Savoy Hotel.

Ted directs the trombone section during a recording session at the Decca studios.

In fact anywhere where there was a chance of a busy gathering of city-bound or homeward-bound commuters, or cinema and theatre queues. A street musician's life, at that particular time (1919) was far from being an easy one.

There were all kinds of hazards including the weather, followed closely by the uncertainty of the 'wages' and, of course, the law.

Playing music in the summer months was not as idyllic as might well be imagined; blowing a trombone on a hot and sunny day could be tiring and very thirsty work. In the winter Ted and his fellow musicians would have to wrap up to the extremes in order to keep the cold at bay.

The imagination does not have to be overstretched to appreciate what it must be like blowing a cold horn, with numb fingers and matchingly-numb lips, and wearing an overcoat at the same time.

During rainy spells of which, naturally, there were many, a cloth cap and a raincoat were a necessity; but even these were not much protection against a heavy lorry which sprayed muddy water from a puddle all over the unfortunate players, and soaked them almost to the skin.

On the plus side, however, the job sometimes paid well. On a good day Ted and his colleagues would collect something like £3 each, which was a great amount of money in those days. Apart from the weather the law, too, was one of the hazards of the job, and Ted and the band of buskers were once charged with causing an obstruction in the Strand.

The incident led to a court appearance at Bow Street Magistrates' Court and, after a plea of guilty to the offence, Ted and the other five musicians were fined 5/- (25p) each.

After that it was back to the streets once more, making music and avoiding the law! Two years later, in 1921, apart from attracting the attentions of the Coventry Street passers-by, Ted and his colleagues were also noted by a man named Joe Banner who had strolled out of his office to listen to the buskers until they had completed their number.

As the musicians finished they were approached. "I'm Joe Banner of Winner Records. How would you like to make a record?" he asked, pointing to the company's offices behind him. At that time radio and television were not regarded as serious public entertainment, but the gramophone was regarded as something of a novelty.

The band was interested in this novel idea of making a record and so, a couple of days later, the players met at the Winner recording studios in the Old Kent Road. They welcomed the recording session for a couple of reasons: in the first place they were about to become involved in a gimmicky new medium and, secondly, the session gave them the chance to get off the streets, and out of the cold!

Not being used to the somewhat new techniques of recording, the band blasted its way through 4 numbers including "O Sole Mio" and Handel's "Largo", blowing its way into a large horn at full volume, just as it would do if it was playing on the streets. The band made 2 records and were paid £2 each. But there were never any royalties ... and no more recording sessions. Not to worry, Ted, better things were on the way!

With this particular band Joe Banner had backed a loser (if he had actually been serious about picking a winner in the first place, that is) but he made plenty of progress himself, for he went on to become an executive for Columbia Records.

Ted is on record as saying that his busking days were a dreary existence and offering nothing in the way of future hopes. But there was a bright spot, and that was that he couldn't get the sack! The horizons of his busking life were limited to the generosity of the listeners in the next street, the meat and 2-veg meal in some back-street cafe (if the day's takings were good) and the uncertainties of the daily share-out over a mug of tea in the evening.

Why did he stand it? The truth, said Ted, was that he knew no better way of living; he was not merely unambitious, but completely apathetic — a strange indictment indeed from a man who was to rise to the very top of his profession.

But, apathy aside, he preferred the life of a busker to being an apprentice coachbuilder at the London General Omnibus Company — the same firm where his father worked. His mother apparently deplored the idea that her son should sink to busking for money, rather than sticking to learning his trade, and she issued Ted with a direct order: "You are not to play anywhere near Wandsworth."

The transparent statement was that she didn't want him playing anywhere near the Heath home in Bassingham Road. Later, when Ted did reach the pinnacle with his band, his mother was to prove his biggest admirer.

The band of buskers often played outside the Queen's Hall Roof Gardens in Langham Place, which was just about the most fashionable nightclub in the London of the early Twenties. Ted's brother Harold played the trumpet there and one day stopped for a word, also introducing him to Jack Hylton. The Queen's Hall band had a problem: one of its trombonists was ill, and Ted was asked to deputise. The upshot of the experience was that it turned out to be a disaster.

Wearing unfamiliar dress clothes the booking also meant playing ragtime music and jazz — a far cry from the busking offerings. The wage was £10 a week (a small fortune) but Ted did not collect the full amount. He lasted only 4 nights for it was suggested to him, kindly and tactfully, that he needed "a little more experience".

Ted's failure did not depress him, for he hadn't expected to succeed. So it was back to busking without brooding over opportunities lost. After all jazz, at that time, was a complete mystery to him, and in any case he felt that busking was infinitely pleasurable to him.

Ted's father's life was obsessed with brass-band music, so it was inevitable that his passion was going to rub off on to his two sons. He taught himself to play all of the brass instruments and, in order to put the borough on the map, suggested that Wandsworth should have its own brass band. And it did, too, with Ted's father nominating himself as its conductor.

But in order for a band to have a conductor, there had to be a band in the first place! And so William George Heath set those wheels in motion by inspiring local tradesfolk, publicans and others of the importance of civic pride and, at the same time, persuading them to part with their money in order to finance the project.

Naturally Ted, albeit reluctantly, was enlisted as a member of the Wandsworth Town Brass Band after much cajoling and bullying from his father, and constant chidings about his lack of ambition. But it was the kind of boost that Ted's ego needed at that particular time, and there was a very different change in his attitude towards music. He had, in fact, reaped the first fruits of his father's insistent sowing.

At that time Ted became a supporter of Fulham Football Club and the pleasure of seeing his team in action at Craven Cottage cost him nothing, for the band played for the crowd's entertainment before the match. In short, this little perk enabled him to watch his favourite team, free of charge, after he had finished playing and had packed away his instrument.

Another boost to his rapidly-growing interest in music came when his brother introduced him to Owen Geary, who was later to become Lt Col Geary of the Royal Artillery, and the conductor of the famous Royal Artillery Band. He proved to be an important stimulus in promoting an interest in bands, which was to prove vital in later years to the young and inexperienced Ted Heath.

During the 2 years that Ted busked for peanuts, his brother Harold was playing in the smart night spots and hotels earning fairly big money. Jazz was becoming a popular novelty and people wanted to dance and forget the horrors of World War One. Therefore any good musician, with a feeling and flair for playing the new syncopated dance music, found himself in a lucrative line of business.

After Harold's previous attempt to give his brother a leg-up had failed miserably, he gave Ted another shove — this time in the direction of an all-coloured American jazz band called the Southern Syncopated Orchestra, which was all set to leave for an engagement in Vienna.

This turned out to be another dismal failure, for the Austrians showed no signs whatsoever of taking to jazz. Ted's salary, when measured in kroner, sounded astronomical. But when it was converted into English currency it amounted to little more than 14/- (70p). The band became morose because of the misfortune, and the players quarrelled and fought amongst themselves — sometimes with knives. After an SOS message to his mother (who called on brass band friends for help) she managed to raise enough money for her son to return home.

A poker game on the train with Ted looking as if he's got a winning hand over Paul Carpenter. Meanwhile, Ted's stage manager, Harry Walters, decides to keep his money in his pocket and sit this one out.

Thankfully, Ted was able to leave Vienna the next morning, only to return home to face an inevitable dressing-down from his mother, with the words: "You ought to put this jazz nonsense out of your head for good and all — there's no future in it". Her words about learning a trade and getting a regular and honest job rang in Ted's ears, but he had to face facts: what trade did he know other than playing the trombone? No, Ted Heath, in his own mind, had no intentions of making a regular pilgrimage to the local Labour Exchange.

Within days of his returning to England he learned that Jack Hylton's orchestra was to play at London's Shaftesbury Theatre. More pleasing still was the fact that Jack remembered Ted's short-lived stay with the Roof Garden band, and booked him for his new orchestra at a salary of £8 a week. He stayed with Hylton for a year before moving on and developing into an eager and ambitious musician, with every new job advancing him in professional status and salary.

By 1925 Ted was earning £45 a week, and his life was very rosy indeed. So rosy, in fact, that he was now rubbing shoulders with other musicians who were to rise into the same orbit — people like Bunny Berigan, Jimmy Dorsey and George Brunies. Yes, life for Ted was now both exciting and rewarding.

All those earlier days of practice had paid off and he was now practising harder and with a far greater will to succeed. Now married to Audrey Keymer, Ted was the father of two children and, as a family man, he bought a house in Wimbledon for £500 and became the owner of his first car.

In 1928 he went to work for Bert Ambrose at the Mayfair Hotel and it wasn't long before he could confirm the whisperings that his boss lived up to his his iron-man reputation. Ted learned that Ambrose was indeed an iron disciplinarian with a penchant for breaking musicians' hearts and being rude to pompous patrons.

He was an absolute stickler for punctuality, insisted that his men wore tailored suits and he allowed no talking on the bandstand; he also had a sharp eye for those who attempted a few words out of the sides of their mouths. He would give them the 'Death Look', and Ted saw many a top musician wilt under it. But, just when Ted felt that he was at the top of his profession, his world fell apart and he felt that all he had worked for was in ruins.

After 8 years of marriage Audrey suddenly fell ill, and within a fortnight she was dead. His sons, Ray (6) and Bobby (5) were sent to boarding school, with Ted suffering many misgivings of conscience because of it. For a year he fell into a state of acute depression, and he turned to spiritualism to help him to accept the loss — spending a great deal of time and money attending seances in an attempt to establish links with the past.

To a point he did find some shreds of hope to carry him through his difficult period, but there was no hope for something that he knew he could not regain. It was a time for Ted to face reality instead of brooding, and his prowess as one of England's leading trombonists was, at that time, more than necessary for his own peace of mind.

But there was an answer to his ills on the horizon, for in 1933 Ted met a young dancer named Moira Tracey — one of 5 members of Buddy Bradley's Ballyhoo Girls, who were the cabaret attraction at the Mayfair, and all of whom Ted gave a lift home in his car after the shows were over.

Moira was the last to be dropped off at her home which, by some strange coincidence or turn of fate, was almost next door to where Ted lived after his first marriage. Their conversations naturally touched on this and, regarding Ted's bereavement, Moira was a good and sympathetic listener; she was understanding and sensed Ted's unhappiness and bewilderment.

Although his intentions were to get to his Nottingham hotel for a wash and a meal before the show, Ted first had to inevitably oblige his autograph-hunting admirers.

The two talked long every night, so it was almost inevitable that they would begin a courtship — with their first date coinciding with the first day's racing at Ascot racecourse. After a somewhat whirlwind romance Ted plucked up the courage to propose marriage to Moira, which she accepted almost without hesitation.

The situation, however, did not appear to be so clean-cut. For a start there was a difference in temperaments; Moira was vivacious whilst Ted was inclined to be taciturn and moody. That was the first obstacle which had to be broken down — and it was. The second barrier was erected by Moira's parents who felt that she was worthy of a better husband than a trombone player who was virtually unknown to them. That apart, he was also a stranger who had been married before and who had 2 growing children.

But their arguments and pleas fell on deaf ears, for Moira's mind was made up. The couple were married on December 16, 1933. Despite all the protestations Moira's parents did attend the wedding and later inspected Oak Cottage, the new house in Copse Hill, Wimbledon, which Ted had bought. They approved of what they saw, and so Ted was accepted into the folds of the Tracey family.

Ted's marriage to Moira was to prove the best thing that ever happened to him; his confidence was restored and he was now playing better than ever before. He was now able to supplement his earnings from Ambrose with radio and recording sessions which increased his income to between £50 and £60 a week.

Like all married couples, however, they had their differences, but most of them were settled by Moira's tolerance. Her tact, patience and encouragement helped to allay many of Ted's self doubts, and he in turn worked to live up to Moira's faith in him. Later, her help was to prove a most vital asset in Ted's dream for his own band becoming a reality.

Ted worked for Ambrose for 8 years, and when he moved from the Mayfair to the Embassy Club he was sacked — but he wasn't surprised. Round about the time when Moira was due to give birth to their son Martin, Ted's playing deteriorated alarmingly. The more he practised to overcome his dilemma the worse it became. Word soon got around and working for Ambrose was already a strain on the nerves, due to his exceptionally high standards. If those standards were not met any musician was out on his ear.

For Ted it was a painful time of reckoning, for the radio and recording dates soon dried up, and so did the bulk of his income. The anxiety of the impending birth had triggered off a lapse of form, and Ted took it all to heart. A feeling of inadequacy took root and it threatened his whole future.

A critical 3 months followed and Ted survived on a couple of engagements a week, with average earnings dramatically reduced to £8 a week or less. It was at this time, when Ted was at the lowest of ebbs, that Sydney Lipton stepped in to act as a saviour, by offering him a job with his orchestra at the Grosvenor House Hotel.

Pictured during an after-concert, get-together at a German air base in Landstuhl are, from left to right, Eric Delaney, Allan Blackburn, Albert Telerico, Derek Boulton and Ted.

The musical grapevine is a very efficient network of communication and Sydney had learned about Ted's loss of form. But, being a musician himself, he knew that the lapse was almost certainly only temporary, and he was prepared to have faith. Ted was only too happy to prove that Sydney's faith in him was justified; he stayed with the band for 4 years during which time he not only hit peak form, but he also developed a new and greater confidence. The end result was that all the private work returned and Ted was back in clover once more.

With the declaration of the Second World War entertainment in the West End came to a very abrupt halt. Ted was in Scotland at the time with the Sydney Lipton band and, at his instigation, Moira and the children joined him. The Lipton orchestra disbanded and the best course of action seemed to be to stay well clear of any large town. Instead, the families went to a remote part of Scotland and, rather pessimistically, waited for the worst to happen. Days and weeks went by, but thankfully nothing did happen.

At this juncture Ted cautiously decided to take a chance and, along with his family, they made their way down to the west of England, steering as far away from London as possible. They stopped at

Blackpool, but at the back of their minds they knew that one of two decisions had to be made: return to the capital to work — if and where possible — or should Ted leave Moira and the children in the north and return alone?

It was really a no-contest situation, despite the sleepless and unhappy nights. They decided that together they would face whatever fate had in store. Separation would be the hardest, and so they all ended up back at Oak Cottage.

Back in the West End Maurice Winnick was the first bandleader to erect a 'Business As Usual' sign outside the Dorchester Hotel, and Ted joined him there. The BBC, too, started a dance band, led by Geraldo, and Ted was asked to join its ranks. He did so because the Geraldo outfit had become the most popular orchestra of the wartime period. It broadcast regularly and brought together families who had been torn apart by the exigencies of war service.

A feature of those broadcasts was a vocal group known as 3 Boys And a Girl. Ted was often one of the 'Boys' — not because he could sing, but because he had been pressed into it by the non-arrival of one or other of the regulars.

Letters from listeners indicated that the broadcasting musicians were greatly appreciated, and the writers addressed the broadcasters as old and trusted friends who, because they were musicians, would understand how much their favourite bands and singers were being missed.

In 1944 Geraldo took his band on a tour of the Middle East, and Ted had the opportunity of feeling the musical pulse of some of the lads who were out there serving with the forces.

But a very curious and poignant thing occurred one night as the band was crossing the Sinai Desert in a bus, and it was halted at a road block. Suddenly the door of the coach was flung open by a sentry. "Geraldo's band, eh?" he commented. "Well don't forget to play 'That Lovely Weekend' tonight!"

On hearing this Ted was now suddenly wide awake. It was the number that he had written, and for which Moira had penned the lyrics. Naturally he hadn't realised just how well known the song was, nor how far it had travelled. As soon as he had a moment to spare he wrote home to Moira, for he knew that she would be every bit as thrilled about it as he was. For the truth is that the number really did have deep and personal memories for both of them.

The number came into being after a weeked visit to the White Rock Pavilion, Hastings, in 1939. Sydney Lipton's band was down there for a booking, and Ted and Moira got up early that morning in order to make the most of the day before the band's engagement in the evening. The truth was that nothing special did happen, except for a swim, a game of golf and an unhurried lunch together.

After playing at the Pavilion they stayed at an hotel for the night, and then took the train back to London the following morning. They both felt that they'd had a marvellous time. When he returned home at 2 am from the Grosvenor, Ted found a note written by Moira on the bedside table, and thanking him in poetic style.

It started: "I haven't said thanks for that lovely weekend . . ." Ted was impressed, but not enough to go along with Moira's suggestion that it might make a very good song. But Moira was not the type who could easily be put off, and the idea stayed with her. When the war started she raised the subject again.

"With all these young men being called up I'm certain that it would make a good parting song," she insisted. Ted backed down and agreed that he thought she had something. After experimenting with various original trombone practice pieces, coupled with a bit of trimming here and there, Ted made the melody fit accurately to the lyrics. But it wasn't an easy ride for the song, for it was turned down by many as "unsuitable" or "we're not interested".

But there was a man who was interested, and the result is one that has been repeated so often in the history of song publishing. In 1941 Geraldo asked each member of his band to pick a favourite tune to make up a broadcast. Ted, obstinate and with a bruised spirit caused by previous rejections, thought that there was nothing to lose when Geraldo asked him for his choice. After a deep breath Ted said: "I Haven't Said Thanks For That Lovely Weekend".

The upshot was that Ted and Moira's song was orchestrated and played on the broadcast, despite certain reservations from Geraldo. Dorothy Carless sang it with such a feeling that it became an immediate hit. But before the broadcast Ted circulated word to all the publishers who had turned down the song, and rubbed in their rejections in order for them to see what they'd missed. Bradbury Wood eventually published the song after hearing it on the broadcast.

After it was published, reactions from listeners was almost instant and sentimental for it touched their hearts, and letters by the dozen poured in from people of all ages. Like most creative people they tend to keep scrapbooks; Ted was no exception to this rule, and the following items are samples which he stuck in that book and treasured.

Dear Mr Geraldo.

Would you be so kind as to let me know the title of the song that the young lady in your band sang last night — and if it is not asking too much would you send me the words, just in case I am unable to get it? The song seems so appropriate at the moment as my husband in the RAF has just sailed for the Middle East.

Dear Miss Carless,

I have never written a fan letter before, but I can't help saying thank you to everyone concerned for "Lovely Weekend". I took it down in shorthand — I think it expresses the feelings of so many of us these days. I have a lovely memory of Easter, and he's now in Libya.

Others wrote to Ted and Moira thanking them, and it wasn't long before the number became the top-selling tune, with recordings by everyone of note in this country and indications of American recognition.

But hopes in that direction were soon to be dashed, as the song was banned by both the NBC and Columbia Broadcasting because the lyric was "too risque". This seemed a remarkable state of affairs considering the nature of some American songs like "Such a Night" and "Teach Me Tonight" which contained lyrics which were explicit rather than merely suggestive.

Ted and Moira even offered to change the lyric, but it didn't help. The song was banned and that was it — such were the strange workings of the American censorship laws at the time. How very different and lax they are today when almost anything and everything goes. However, they were not to be denied their success in the States, for Moira penned another poem for the forces who were returning to civilian life. She came up with "I'm Gonna Love That Guy", and once again Ted wrote the music.

This one really was a hit in the US and was recorded by Perry Como, Dinah Shore, Dick Haymes, Benny Goodman and a whole host of artists. In fact, on one particular visit to the ABC studios in New York, Ted found 13 different recordings of the number.

Naturally there were some very big royalties from the 2 songs and they still kept drifting in over a long period — especially from "I'm Gonna Love That Guy", which enjoyed a new lease of life when it was featured in a film and was sung by Betty Grable.

The success of their songs came from the fact that the lyrics had been written to fit a topical situation. Many of the big hits over the years have been in the same vein, and aspiring songwriters have followed the same course. Success, really, is all a matter of being the first to get a toe in the door. Ted and Moira had made the opening; they were successful — especially Moira — who saw her name on many song copies as lyric writer.

But whichever of the two had the most success was an irrelevance. What became relevant was that the seeds had been sown for the creation of Ted's dream band — a musical institution and, to a great extent a musical family, that was to burst on to the British music scene like nothing before it, and which was later to conquer the world.

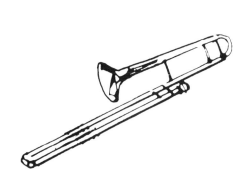

CHAPTER THREE

The Dream Becomes a Reality

 When the Ted Heath band made its debut in 1945 it lost virtually no time at all in becoming one of the most talked-about musical outfits — and not only in this country either. Ted soon won the admiration of the American leaders, even though all of whom were legends in their own right.

In the interests of their own self-preservation, it seemed the natural thing to do that the likes of Kenton, Ellington and Basie should keep their fingers on the pulse of the Heath band. For this was one British outfit that was really going places. And they knew it, too!

The Heath band represented a complete musical institution, equipped with the best musicians and music-scoring brains in Britain. Its main driving force came from within the depths of the brass section, with every member being both an accompaniest as well as a celebrated soloist.

The precision of the section work, the full impact of the ensemble and the general taste in presentation set a remarkably high standard, and one which was never to be equalled let alone beaten.

In the days when the big bands were in vogue it was the name of the Ted Heath band which represented all that was best in British dance and swing music. And yet this was something of a contradiction in terms, really, for there are a great number of dancers and dance-hall devotees who will argue that Ted's outfit was one that could not be danced to without great difficulty — if at all.

The main reason for this, perhaps, was not because his playing style was too advanced, but by the time that everyone in the various palais' up and down the country had crowded in front of the stage to watch and listen to his all-star line-up, there just wasn't any room left on the floor in which to dance!

It seemed that all who attended Ted's appearances were quite content to stand, watch, listen and soak up everything that his multi-talented band could offer.

In those days the word 'talent' meant exactly that; it wasn't applied lightly and it certainly was not lavished upon someone who was not the complete master of his instrument. Entrance to a big band — especially Ted Heath's — had to be earned by way of a thorough musical knowledge, and the application of that knowledge had to be proved by the virtuosity of both the musician and his instrument.

Every single member of the Heath band was a complete master — a craftsman of his instrument. There was no easy way to become a member of this outfit for, as Britain's premier band, it was universally considered amongst the musical fraternity to be, maybe jokingly, a dead-man's shoes job.

Every musician was hand-picked by Ted to do a special and specific job in the band, which was the main reason why his outfit always looked and sounded so united and precise. The Heath philosophy was a simple one; he did not just want an outfit of first-class musicians, he wanted a first-class musical family.

The true adage that there is never a second chance to make a first impression was certainly true in the case of yours truly when I first saw the Ted Heath outfit on that memorable night back in 1953. Struck with awe and admiration, and no doubt with an air of naivety, my own personal observation was two-fold. Here was a band destined to go places, and with all the famous venues in many countries of the world offering it the chance to do just that.

After all, those Sunday-night swing sessions at the London Palladium not only attracted all the big theatrical agents from this country, but also impressarios from outside Britain — people who would, if they could, present Ted with the opportunity to put his band on the centre stage of the world's most famous auditoriums.

The second observation was that Ted had assembled a band so rich in playing talents, and so strong in depth in backroom musical arrangers and orchestrational brain power, that even at the age of 14 it was not difficult to deduct that Ted Heath and His Music was light years ahead of its time. No disrespect is intended to all the other many fine bands which were around at the time, but, putting them alongside the concerts, the recordings and the overwhelming appeal to the masses of British big-band enthusiasts, Ted's band was, quite simply different.

It was an institution which was worthy of anything that the rest of the world could offer. Its limitations were endless, and the overall feeling was that this was a band which could scale the greatest of heights. History went on to prove that it did just that. So it was with a deeply personal sense of satisfaction that my early observations proved to be correct.

Blasts From the Past

Wally Smith

Ric Kennedy

Ronnie Hughes

Three of the men who were so vitally important in maintaining the standard of Ted Heath's instantly-recognisable brass section. It was this sound which was to carry his outfit through to the highest echelons of big-band swing music.

By virtue of Ted's massive appeal, both in Britain and America, every member of his band was held in the highest esteem. His four trumpeters were the band's crowning glory with Bobby Pratt, Bert Ezzard, Duncan Campbell and Eddie Blair featuring in both solo passages and as a team. In unison they blew with complete understanding and precision, rising above the rest of the band in a show of force. In solo mode each man played with an individuality of approach and a contrast of execution.

The trombone section was as talented in its own right as the trumpet section, with one man from this unit who will always be remembered with the Ted Heath band — then and since. That man is Don Lusher. He was an instant hit with the audiences right from the start of his career with Ted's band, and his professional attitude to his work on stage, coupled with his gentlemanly demeanour off it, makes it so understandable to see why the man is so popular and such an influence to the younger players of today.

To see and hear him play his own composition, "Lush Slide", was a comparative to watching an artist at work on a canvas. To listen to his control over what was a very difficult number to play was something akin to the feeling one gets when touching the richness of silk. That richness was the beautiful and flawless tone that came from his instrument.

27

At the time of my early obsession with Ted's band, and my unstinting admiration for his musicians, he also had two other members in the band who were extremely popular — drummer Ronnie Verrell and bassist Johnny Hawksworth.

Hawksworth at that time was arguably the best double bass player in Britain. Just as Don got all that he wanted from his trombone, so Johnny did with the bass. In his hands the huge instrument was like a dummy, with Johnny as the musical ventriloquist. In short, he could almost make it talk to him! The big tone and sure-fingered accuracy, which he displayed through his solo works, provided the drive from way back as he underlined the whole ensemble.

Just in case there are any readers who are wondering whatever became of him since the Heath band split up, and why it is that he is not an integral part of the Don Lusher-directed band of today, the reason is that these days Johnny spends most of his time working and commuting between Sydney and Singapore — quite a drag from there to these shores for a few one-night stands, wouldn't you agree?

What might be of some interest to note is that to those people who have a penchant for television signature tunes, and who thought that the first series of "George and Mildred", back in the early Seventies, contained one of the catchiest tunes around actually came from the pen of Johnny — as indeed did the eight-notes jingle which accompanied the graphic at the beginning of every Thames Television programme.

There were many good drummers around in those days, too, but Ronnie Verrell was considered to be in a class of his own — at least as far as this country was concerned. He was, and still is, an exciting man to watch, with all the ingredients of genius to his credit: calm at the right time, explosive when it matters the most and ultimate timing at the precise second.

In his early days Ronnie could best be described as a cross-breed drummer with veins of similarity to Gene Krupa, Shelley Mann and even Buddy Rich all rolled into one. Yet beneath it all there was his very own individual streak of not wishing to be tarred with the same brush as his American counterparts.

Ronnie, however, was a clear-cut showman who appealed very much to the public on his tours of the United States with the band. His faked bouts of nonchalance, only to suddenly come alive again with a dynamic outburst of drumnastics, had his audiences sweating almost as much as himself.

Devotees of Ted Heath's music will know that the main criteria of his success was that he had no need to rely on the material of other bands, or the compositions of other bandleaders. His secret? It was simply that he had great strength in depth. His musical library consisted of countless quantities of original material, written and arranged by a backroom staff which was as strong in talent as the men who Ted fronted out on stage.

From within these ranks Ted employed people like Reg Owen, Ron Roullier, Ralph Dollimore, Johnny Keating and Norman Stenfalt. And just to show their own brand of versatility, away from the Heath empire, both Reg Owen and Johnny Keating reached the hit parade with their own compositions — Johnny with the theme from the highly-successful television series "Z Cars" and Reg with "Manhattan Spiritual".

Another success factor of the Ted Heath band were the singers, who were very much part and parcel of this truly great organisation. In the post-Paul Carpenter days it was the sight and sound of Dickie Valentine and Dennis Lotis which set the girls' hearts fluttering, while the lads did anything (and almost everything) to 'click' with Lita Roza. Of the three it was Dickie who was to emerge as the most popular.

After he discovered that his hero Johnnie Ray was in the audience, singer Dickie Valentine almost collapsed afterwards with excitement.

He had personality, and a good singing voice to go with it. Needless to say that if he hadn't then he would never have stood a chance with Ted. He also had a fairy-tale entrance into the world of the big-band business. At one time he had been employed as a page-boy at the London Palladium, but after getting the sack he took up singing lessons with British star Bill O' Connor, who also sponsored him.

After only six weeks as a professional he was given the break of a lifetime when he was asked by Ted to join his band as one of its singers. At the time Dickie was only 20, short in height and with dark, curly hair. Although he was a little on the plump side it didn't hinder his appeal to his flocks of female admirers.

Dickie didn't concentrate too much on crooning or straight singing. Instead, he tried to broaden his sphere. He had a good eye and a well-trained ear for impersonating the top singers of the day. What's more he had the talent to be able to carry out those impersonations successfully, and Ted allowed him both room and scope to develop his variety style.

His speciality was a brilliant take-off of Johnnie Ray — reputed to be Dickie's idol. So successful were his impersonations of Johnnie that word soon got back to the American star. At one particular concert, at the London Palladium, he turned up to watch Dickie in action, and to see what kind of a job he was making of his (Ray's) image.

Ted knew of the presence of the distinguished visitor in the audience, but Dickie had no idea. And Ted didn't tell him either!

In complete and blissful ignorance he ripped into his impersonation of Johnnie and the audience's wild applause almost brought the house down. Afterwards, when he was told that his idol had been sitting in the front stalls, Dickie almost collapsed with excitement. Later, the two men met up, and the American praised his imitator on a first-rate job.

Dickie made many records with Ted's band, and also when he left to go solo. The most notable of his successes were "Broken Wings", The Finger of Suspicion" and "All the Time and Everywhere". He was rarely out of work, but sadly he was killed in a road crash in 1971.

Along its ever-progressive path the band sold a fantastic number of records. These sales naturally put Ted's band in a much sought-after position, and in that same debut year the management of the London Palladium decided to stage an experimental series of Sunday night swing sessions. Some experiment!

The venture snowballed into one of the most acclaimed and spectacular bi-weekly concert dates in the country. The sessions went on for many years and Ted took full advantage of the opportunity that had landed in his lap.

The concerts, 109 in all, gave the band the chance to play many of its more ambitious arrangements which, though less suitable to its style when playing for dancing, served to illustrate its tremendous power when given the setting of the concert platform.

After the 100th London Palladium concert there was a very special surprise in store for Ted backstage, in the form of a silver inscribed tray.

However, it did not come from the theatre management, as might well have been expected, but from the lads in the band — his beloved family of musicians. The inscription read:

> *"A tribute to a gentleman. A token of thanks, in silver, to TED HEATH a great leader. From all the boys in the band, 1945-1954, on the occasion of his 100th concert at the London Palladium."*

When Ted's band stood as a colossus over the British big-band scene the Palladium concerts can point to the previous stuggles and uphill battle. And the ultimate success.

The Decca Record Company lost no time at all in realising the ever-increasing potential of Ted's outfit, when it installed recording apparatus in the theatre for a series of 'live' concerts which were later released on LPs — cassettes and CDs being very much commodities for the future.

In this respect he was not only the ambassador of this country's big-band swing scene, but he was also the father figure who won the admiration of all who either worked with him, or for him.

Ted's notion of having a band of his own really began to take root when he was returning home from the Middle East in 1944. Geraldo had already flown home ahead, and the rest of the band took the more leisurely route by sea. In organising band concerts for them on the journey Ted was, unconsciously, emulating his father, for he had watched him issuing instructions to musicians in the brass band. Ted also took to authority and enjoyed the feeling of being the leader of the band . . . in Geraldo's absence!

After that the idea gnawed away at him, and the more he regarded it the more logical and inevitable it seemed. At that time Ted was at the zenith of his powers as a musician. He knew that as the years went by he could only diminish; he was then in his 40s and dance music was a young man's profession. But if he did start a band what kind would it be, and what music would it play?

In his mind there was an ideal: a beautifully-disciplined, precisional and powerful band like the Glenn Miller Orchestra. Ted was convinced even at that stage that the only way to match that sort of performance was by hiring the very best musicians, regardless of the cost, giving them thrilling orchestrations and offering them the kind of music that would challenge them to produce their best.

Ted's dream was that his band would be better than any yet heard in Europe; it would take the country by storm (which it did) much as

31

Miller's had captured America. Ted had the experience, and he knew how it could be done. But dreams weren't enough and the venture would cost a lot of money.

By good chance he had received a royalty cheque from sales of "That Lovely Weekend", and so that gave the dreams a fair proportion of financial substance. Of course part of the money belonged to Moira, but she had philosophically accepted what was indeed the inevitable; her share of the royalties was, consequently, added to the investment.

But even in the light of this there were problems. The war was still on and no one seemed to be interested in hearing what Ted's theories were on bands — no one, that is, except Douglas Lawrence, a young BBC producer. To Ted's astonishment the man listened and offered him a broadcast for several months ahead, in order to give Ted the time to complete his arrangements. That then meant searching for the right men — they had to be the right men. Finally, after a lot of hassle tracing them and tracking them down, Ted got most of the men he needed.

He paid top prices for his arrangements and offered the musicians more than the established BBC rate for the job, solely as an inducement for them to take the engagement seriously. They did take the offer seriously, and so the broadcast was transmitted on Saturday lunchtime, August 29, 1944. Despite an obvious-sounding boob by one of the players, coupled with Ted's conviction of a failure at the first hurdle, the session was a successful one and, to confirm this, the BBC gave the band more broadcasts.

In 1945 another BBC producer, Pat Dixon, sent for Ted and offered him a complete series of broadcasts. These had, in fact, been projected some time earlier as Ted learned later through the BBC grapevine. The

Among the many who called to pay their compliments to Ted are top British artists Petula Clark and Lonnie Donegan.

new series was called "Top Ten" and was initially scheduled to run for 6 weeks; it ran for 27 weeks, thus underlining the measure of its popularity.

Dixon saw to it that the BBC paid an extra fee to cover the special orchestrations which Ted demanded, and he continued to pay his musicians extra money from his own pocket. And Moira's, too! For without her co-operation and self-sacrifice it would not have been possible to carry through his ambitious schemes.

The abrupt metamorphosis from trombone player with Geraldo to bandleader was not easy, and Ted felt that to command his wants he had to question, reason, ask politely and suggest. Fortunately the musicians liked his musical policy and were tractable enough.

Many later became famous in their own right after they had left Ted's band. Trumpeter Eddie Calvert rose to international fame with his hit record "Oh Mein Papa", Paul Carpenter, Ted's first vocalist and compere, became an accomplished actor, Kenny Baker rose to great heights with his own Baker's Dozen and guitarist Vic Lewis went on to lead one of Britain's most popular orchestras.

Ted was later to confirm what must have been obvious to a great many people: although he was the leader of a very fine band, he was also very reluctant to be in the spotlight, and was therefore quite nervous when it came to fronting his men. It was the only aspect of bandleading that he didn't enjoy, and so he therefore left all the announcing to Paul Carpenter in the early days.

Ted was conscious of his slight Cockney accent, and was only at his happiest when working on a broadcast or in a recording studio. In his mind was the belief that people were more interested in the band than its leader.

The necessary impetus for Ted's future plans were given a great boost with the arrival in this country in 1944 of Glenn Miller and his band. Again, through the BBC grapevine, he learned of Miller's rather hush-hush visit and plans by the corporation to broadcast a concert by his band from the Bedford Corn Exchange.

Ted hopped on a train from London to Bedford and managed to gatecrash the concert. Later, with the help of a BBC friend, he was introduced to the man himself and was not only childishly proud that he had met him, but he was also infected with a kind of Glenn Miller fever.

Back in London Ted found that the American was staying at the Mount Royal Hotel, and he went to see him. The two men once again met up backstage a few days later at the Queensbury Club (later to become the London Casino), only this time it was to prove to be the last occasion.

They talked of many things including trombone playing, orchestrations, and Ted's bandleading aspirations. Glenn suggested meeting again after his return from Europe, and before he went back to America.

He then wished Ted good luck with his dreams for his own band before departing on his ill-fated trip to Paris on December 14, 1944. The world now knows that Glenn never arrived at his destination, and the tragedy was not only a great loss to the dance-music world, but also a personal loss to every musician who ever had the good fortune to meet him and know him.

Glenn Miller's successful formula was the basis for Ted's aspirations when he came to form his own orchestra.

The "Top Ten" series of broadcasts put the Ted Heath band on the map, and there were many letters of appreciation to prove it. Critics praised his style as the best thing to happen to British dance music for years.

The band caught the interest of musicians, too, because of its progressive policy. But there were also those who inevitably resented his ambitious plans.

Ted was using all the best musicians available so it was understandable that some bandleaders were going to regard him as a musical interloper.

But apart from following the well-worn path of other leaders, by taking musicians from established bands, those same men wanted to work for Ted because he was offering them something in addition to good money — he was giving them the chance of a renewed interest in their livelihood.

Ted left Geraldo's employ on VE Day, in 1945. The time had now arrived to put half measures in the past, for in order to run his own band as a full-time concern it had to be done properly. There were many risks involved, but then Ted knew that. So, too, did Moira. They talked long and hard, with both realising that the whole venture would be a gamble, with very high stakes.

Although he knew that he was committing the livelihood and well-being of his family with that gamble for the future, Ted was convinced that the "Top Ten" broadcasts had put his music on the map. After all, he reasoned, how many new bands had started off life with a long BBC radio series tucked under its belt.

With Geraldo's words of "You'll regret it" giving him a far from optimistic send-off to his new career, Ted decided that he had to have an influential business address to work from, so he opened up an office at 23 Albermarle Street, Mayfair, at a weekly rent of £20. He hired a secretary, furnished the place with a desk, office fittings and a typewriter and also bought a car of an appearance to match his new status. But he was stung with his purchase, and had to pay dearly when

2 weeks later he discovered that the engine had a cracked cylinder block.

He also spent well on band uniforms, music stands and a whole library of specially-commissioned orchestrations, as he prepared for his band to make its touring debut at what was then considered to be the plum venue in the country — Belle Vue, Manchester. Arrangements were made for the band to travel north in a railway sleeping car, rather than suffer with the discomforts of motor coaches which lurched through the night with their loads of cold, cramped and weary musicians.

Telephone calls to the Belle Vue manager in the days prior to the opening engagement, however, brought the disturbing news that advance bookings were not going too well. At this point Ted was not unduly worried. His band had thousands of fans, via the broadcasts, who were just waiting their chance to see and hear his outfit in the flesh. It would be all right on the night, Ted thought.

He assured himself that once the doors were open the crowds would flock in. It was sheer self-delusion, for the band played to a mere sprinkling of folk in a half-empty hall, and with the excellence of its efforts bouncing back on them in mocking echoes.

That first booking proved to be a financial loss: Ted's share of the takings amounted to £57 — less, in fact, than what the train fares had cost. To make matters worse Ted had promised the band members £10 each for the engagement. Returning home on the train he did some drastic mental arithmetic, for he had nothing in the way of private funds to cover the misfortune of the night. In short, he simply had not considered that the evening could possibly be a flop.

But a flop it had been, and so Ted gathered his men together and explained to them the pathetic amount that was in the kitty. "There's only one thing to do, fellas," he said. "I'll have to share the £57 between you." They accepted in good grace, but their confidence was shaken just as much as Ted's was.

He slept little that night on the journey back to London as he searched for a solution. And all the time it was questions, questions and more questions. What had happened to all those youngsters who had written to tell him that his band was the greatest? Had the event been sufficiently publicised? If he couldn't pull in the crowds in such a large and thickly-populated area as Manchester, what would happen in other parts of the country? And finally, if the earning power remained as low as this how would the musicians in the band react?

In the weeks to follow all Ted could offer them was the occasional broadcast and the odd, and anything but lucrative, engagement that happened to come along. The musicians, most of which were family men, started to drift away. All were apologetic and regretted the break as much as Ted, for they were all at great pains to point out that they got a great kick out of playing Ted's kind of music. But . . .

A stroke of luck came Ted's way shortly after, in June of that year, and without it his band would almost certainly have foundered and possibly died. The break came in the shape of Salvador "Toots" or "Tutti" Camarata who had arrived in this country to collect together a band and oversee the arrangements for a film.

A former trumpet player with the Jimmy Dorsey orchestra, Tutti Camarata was the man responsible for the Dorsey band winning no less than 12 gold records. For it was Tutti who had written the arrangements for numbers such as "Amapola", "The Breeze and I" and a whole string of other numbers.

Camarata wasn't the kind of man to go overboard with enthusiasm about anything, but he made no bones about the fact that he was impressed with Ted's outfit, and so he booked it. The wages for the job, Tutti enlarged, would be paid on a daily scale: £5 a man for each 3-hour session. It proved to be a lifesaver. But there was a devastating drawback to it all. Ted wasn't needed — only his band. Tutti explained: "I'm sorry, Ted, but I shan't be needing you. I have to conduct the score myself. Ted felt as though he had just been punched in the stomach. "You can't do that," he yelled. "It's my band!"

He was in England to act as musical director on a film called "London Town", which was to be made at the Shepperton film studios. Apparently the J. Arthur Rank Organisation was going to show the Americans — particularly MGM — how to make a musical. Fat chance! The film was an all-time flop.

The band nicknamed Shepperton studios 'The Mint' because it was not unusual for them to be there at the studios early in the morning and not getting away until perhaps two o' clock the following morning — having picked up, probably, four session fees.

And don't forget that right after the war, when people had only recently been demobbed, this was great money.

Incidentally, at the time of the shooting of "London Town", Ted's band line-up was: Harry Roche, Laddie Busby, Harry Letham, Dave Goldberg, Jimmy Coombes, Jack Parnell, Reg Owen, Les Gilbert, Johnnie Gray, Norman Stenfalt, Ronnie Scott, Stan Roderick, Alan Franks, Dave Shand, Charlie Short, Kenny Baker and Jack Bentley.

The saxophone section of the mid-40s, with (from left to right): Dave Shand, Reg Owen, Les Gilbert, Johnnie Gray and Ronnie Scott.

Camarata acknowledged Ted's position and a compromise was agreed. The band was credited in the film under Ted's name; Tooti would conduct and Ted would receive a small fee as his " sleeping partner". Thankfully the arrangement worked and, as far as Ted was concerned, the experience of working with Tutti proved to be nothing short of educational. He was a musician of the highest ability and someone who knew exactly what he wanted musically and, more importantly, precisely how to get it. The band made great strides under his direction, and Ted stood in the wings throughout those weeks of filming watching and digesting his technique.

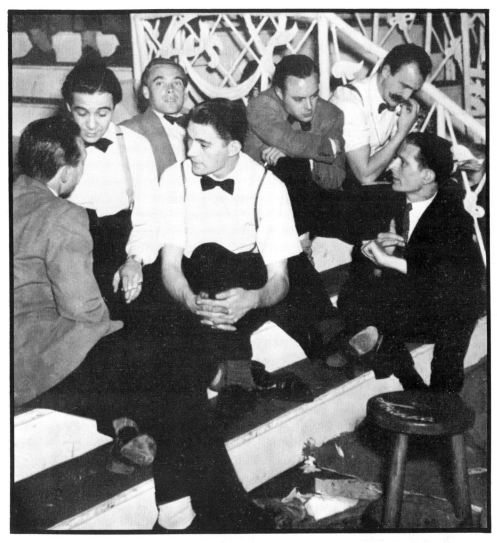

Film work invariably meant long waiting periods while camera angles were explored, lighting readjusted and scripts carefully timed. While all this went on Ted's musicians had to sit around and wait until their services were required.

During that time the last thing that went through his mind was the feasibility that 11 years later he would actually be playing a starring role in "It's a Wonderful World", with Ted's name up there in the credits alongside such artists as Kathleen Harrison, George Cole and Terence Morgan. Even less was the possibility that he would ever get the chance to take his band to America, or to play in front of the Royal Family at 2 Command Performances.

Just as an interjection here ... food for thought if you like. The American film companies, naturally, lost no time at all in making biographies devoted to their revered dance-band heroes such as "The Fabulous Dorseys", "The Benny Goodman Story" and of course "The Glenn Miller Story". And although they may very well have been devised and produced along low-budget lines, to the cinemagoer this mattered not one iota.

They were all box-office hits and the takings more than recouped the initial outlay for the productions. So much so that the companies involved all received pats on the back and probably had more than a few celebratory drinks to toast their respective successes.

But what of the British film industry? What about "The Ted Heath Story"? What indeed! At the time when this country had a band which was every bit as equal to any of those in America, all that the British film-industry honchoes could do was to huff, puff, discuss, dither, delay and finally abandon any ideas it might have had with a misinformed, "Well it wouldn't have made good box-office anyway" The question is, how the hell could they possibly know — they never even gave the project a shot?

In his first year as a full-time bandleader Ted was heavily in debt, and seeing little or no way out of his difficulties. He was earning less than in his days as a rank-and-file instrumentalist — much less — with his musicians taking home more from the proceeds than he was. But Ted realised that economies were not possible: he had an all-star band and he knew that he couldn't succeed with inferior, less-expensive musicians. His band's appeal at that time was to a relatively-small minority of the population — the young swing fans. What Ted needed was a firm, yet semi-permanent engagement; he required a venue where a few thousand of the band's fans could be brought together under one roof. Preferably in London.

In his desperation Ted stumbled upon an idea which was to turn out not only to be a brainwave, but an undisputable milestone. In order to set the wheels of his idea in motion he took his drummer, Jack Parnell, to one side. "Val Parnell is your uncle — right?" asked Ted. "Do you think we might ask him if we could try out some Sunday concerts at the London Palladium?"

Jack looked doubtful to say the very least, but he agreed with his boss that there could be no harm in trying. Val was approached and surprisingly didn't turn the idea down. But he did have certain reservations over what he'd heard about swing fans, and their rather noisy way of showing their appreciation. Val said he'd heard about their jitterbugging and even destructive forms of exhibitionism, and he didn't want his beloved Palladium being disrupted by such unruly behaviour.

Ted argued that his fans were not like that, and so Val was persuaded to allow the band fortnightly concerts. But on one condition. Any damage caused to carpets and fittings would have to be paid for out of Ted's pocket. Ted agreed, and the famous Sunday swing sessions, which were to eventually become a part of British big-band folklore, began on December 9, 1945, and continued right up until the time when the Palladium was given over to commercial television.

CHAPTER FOUR

Swinging Sunday Nights

 It was a cold and damp December Sunday when Ted assembled his band for rehearsals at the Palladium; it was an experiment, and a desperate one at that. This was the chance he needed to prove that his fans would put their money where his faith was — on his band. Little did he realise that his last-ditch idea was to become a milestone in British big-band history.

What he did realise, however, was that this was one of the many theatres outside of which he played as a busker. This time, though, it was different. This time he was top of the bill *inside*. The band did more than a hundred concerts at the world-famous venue and they were a sell-out right from the start.

And as a matter of reassurance to Val Parnell, with regards to the alleged hearsay behaviour of the swing fans, Ted never had to pay a penny for any damage!

Which was perhaps as well, for the cost of hiring the theatre was very heavy and the margin for profit was small. In fact, over the years those Sunday swing sessions turned out to be the least profitable of all the Sunday concerts which Ted and his band were ever involved in anywhere.

This, however, turned out to be a relatively minor inconvenience, when all things were taken into consideration. For example, there was

> ## *Ted's mother barely missed a concert. "That's my boy up there," she would say to the young swing fans seated near her*

With the setting of the London Palladium stage, Ted leads his all-star band in one of the famous Sunday Night Swing Sessions. Those concerts have now become part of British big-band folklore.

the prestige of playing at the London Palladium along with the atmosphere of the place — almost as if it had itself accepted both the band and its music. The audiences warmed to their surroundings and the concerts took on something in the nature of a fortnightly reunion of friends. Especially one — Ted's mother.

She hardly missed one of those 100-odd concerts, although it's open to debate whether she developed any real understanding of the music which the band played. But Ted's mother delighted savouring the fact that it was her son   who was up there on the stage, and in the limelight. At the age of 80 she would sit among the young swing fans applauding everything that the band did more vigorously than anyone else, and at times she couldn't stop her pleasure from spilling over.

"That's my boy up there," she'd cry, nudging the occupant of the next seat. "Ted Heath — he's my son!" It's unlikely that anyone believed her, but that still did nothing to quell her pleasure.

Probably the most moving of all the Palladium concerts was the 100th occasion that Ted and the band played at the theatre. There was an emotional feeling in the air that night, right from the time when the curtain went up at the start of the show, and the boys in the band presented Ted with a beautiful engraved silver tray.

They also presented Moira with an enormous bouquet of flowers and a jewel case with a gold trombone charm inside, signed *"With love and affection from the "Orchestra Wives"*.

The show ended with many ex-band members playing alongside those of the present line-up, with each signing off to "Farewell Blues" and finally leaving Ted alone on the stage. It was, for the maestro, a wonderful memory of an equally-wonderful evening.

However, the memories of those successful Palladium nights still did not make the band a permanently-viable proposition. The money which it earned seemed to drain away in covering all kinds of incidental expenses. The transport bills, for example, were very heavy with most of the profits finding their way into the pockets of coach proprietors or railway coffers.

Ted knew that he had a good and successful band, but he always seemed to be struggling for survival. With the threat of extinction staring him in the face, he still could not face up to the fact that a bandleader also had to be a musical caterer. But he was soon to learn that unless he satisfied the tastes of the broad masses of people, then he had no real chance of survival.

When he took his band to play its first appearance at the Hammersmith Palais his programme consisted of an almost unrelieved programme of jazz music, which was much to the pleasure of the hordes of youngsters who crowded in front of the bandstand. But the proprietor of the Palais was concerned that too many patrons were sitting it out far too often on the sidelines.

Just how popular the attraction of Ted Heath and His Music really was is depicted in this picture, on one of the many occasions when he and the band played at the Hammersmith Palais

44

He sent a message down to Ted suggesting that his customers might enjoy a waltz. Ted's reply was terse and straight to the point, saying that as long as he had a band he would *never* play a waltz. He also said that if the owner didn't like it then he would take his band out.

Ted was later the first to admit that his stance on this occasion was the wrong one to take. His band was there to play for dancing, and it was up to him to please those dancers. Yet it took him years, and perhaps thousands of pounds, to learn that lesson. He stuck to his principle of paying his musicians very good money, not a weekly salary but a set sum for each engagement — which was something in the region of £9.

It was more than Ted could really afford; it left nothing to cover him against loss on a bad evening, and it was considerably more than any other bandleader was paying at that time.

However, in the summer of 1946, the band was given a 3-week season at the Winter Gardens, Blackpool, which proved to be an annual life-saver for many years. It was at this point when the signs began to show that the band was in bigger demand than ever before. However, it was not before the BBC, which had previously been instrumental in getting the band started with those Top Ten broadcasts, suddenly turned its back on Ted Heath and His Music.

The BBC's Listener Research organisation had established that Ted's music was deplored by middle-aged listeners, and it fell at a time when the minor post-war boom in the dance-band business collapsed. But Ted was adamant that he had no intentions of allowing the BBC to dictate his musical policy.

A star drops in to say 'Hello'

British film actress Jean Simmons, a devoted fan of the band, pays Ted a visit in his dressing room at the London Palladium.

Blackpool Panorama

This picture shows only a part of the enormous crowd which gathered to hear Ted's band during its summer seasons at the Winter Gardens, Blackpool. Two-tier balconies on all sides of the ballroom are equally packed with holiday-making music fans.

Even if he had wanted to commercialise his style of orchestration, by putting the accent on simple melody, he had virtually no vocalists who were capable of bearing the brunt of long series of popular song choruses.

Paul Carpenter, for example, was a better compere than he was a vocalist, and Ted's only other singer was Jack Parnell who specialised, with some success, in swingy Americanised ditties.

But Ted believed in fate, however grim the situation seemed. He reckoned that something would always turn up if he could hang on long enough. And it did, in the shape of a Mr Domenico, a restaurant proprietor in Scotland. In what appeared to indicate some purpose in the confusion of life's interests, this man held the key to Ted's problem.

With the running of the band soaking up resources at an alarming rate, the royalties from Ted and Moira's successful songs "That Lovely Weekend" and "I'm Gonna Love That Guy" were spent almost as soon as they arrived. It appeared to be one thing after another, for at that time the lease holders of 23 Albermarle Street announced that they were disposing of the lease, and unless Ted and the other tenants were prepared to buy it they would have to move out.

Like Ted, the other tenants, Eric Robinson and George Melachrino, did not want to give up the premises as they all considered that they would lose business by it. Not only that, but finding alternative offices would prove to be even more costly. They decided that they would buy the lease and stay . . . somehow.

Mr Domenico had 2 attractive daughters who were both aspiring songwriters, and he persuaded Ted to listen to the girls singing their songs. Ted realised that they had promise, but from his own experience he knew the difficulties they faced in persuading the Tin Pan Alley experts to put a song into print. Mr Domenico was warned of this but defiantly he offered to open his own concern and publish the songs himself.

Ted broke the man's leg gently by pointing out to him that printing songs was the easy part; the hardest was finding artists to record them and then promoting the finished product into the "hit" class, with no guarantees whatsoever of success.

Mr Domenico heeded the warning but Ted, too, had also learned from the discussion. The man's daughters, plus Ted's shrewd thinking, started a chain of thought that was to affect the band's future policy. More and more Ted was becoming conscious that his band just did not have enough appeal to reach the widest of audiences.

He was still seething with the BBC, yet he was in a Catch 22 situation: he did not agree that to popularise dance music was to cut out musical ambition and make it secondary to singers, but he knew that there was a middle road he could take to attract more customers without losing his musical ideals.

In order to reach a personal compromise Ted decided to hire a vocalist — an unknown who could be gradually developed within the band. Lydia Domenico was that vocalist, with a change of surname to Macdonald. There was an outcry from the band's supporters because they thought that her engagement would be out of character with the band. But having chosen his course, Ted stuck to it, and was to benefit immensely from Lydia's father. For on hearing of his plight over the Albermarle Street lease, Mr Domenico lent Ted £2,500 to take care of the problem.

Lydia didn't stay with the band for very long, which was hardly surprising. Coming from a comfortable home like she did, touring as a vocalist was not as congenial as she had hoped. Not unsurprisingly she became quickly disillusioned with travelling around the country, often being forced to sleep in her stage clothes on overnight journeys en route for the next date, and yet being expected to face an audience looking fresh and elegant.

Certainly there was no glamour for Lydia in touring with the band and, to Ted's dismay, she returned to her home in Scotland.

If nothing else the departure proved to be a setback to Ted's plan of nurturing a promising singer, for he was still insolvent and clinging to the hope that the band might yet fight its way through the bad patch. But there was a morale booster on the way, via the Variety Artists' Benevolent Society, which informed Ted that his band had been chosen to play at the Royal Command Performance in October, 1948.

Ted was both thrilled and more than a little frightened of the honour accorded to him and his band. At the forefront of his mind was the thought that his music was likely to sound brash and undignified, especially in the starch and elegance of such a regal occasion as this.

However, he was boosted by the knowledge that the Queen (then Princess Elizabeth) and her younger sister, Princess Margaret, were both fans of his music.

Ted's wisdom and self-belief prevailed in choosing his musical programme. He reckoned that the best approach was simply to be himself. His band had been chosen with the full knowledge of its style, and he knew that the various acts on the bill had to be approved by the Sovereign. Consequently, the band played much that was typical and true to its style, although the more advanced and ambitious arrangements were not included.

The reception which the band received, from both the royalty and the august audience, convinced Ted that he and his men had done the business.

Early the following year Syd Green, a music publisher, called at Ted's office bringing with him a very nervous young man. When Ted spoke to him he had to clear his throat a few times before his vocal chords responded. He was, in fact, completely in awe of Ted. "This is Dickie Bryce. I believe he's just what your band needs," enthused Syd. The young man had been a call-boy at the London Palladium and used to tell Canadian Bill O' Connor, who was lead singer in the show "Follow the Girls", about his ambitions of becoming a star.

Ted fronts the band at the Royal Command Performance in October, 1948

The reception which Ted received, from both royalty and the august audience, convinced him that his band had done the business

Ted's mind was once again ticking over: he'd noted that the girl fans of the band far outnumbered the males — probably on account of all the eligible young men who played in it. He needed a singer to keep those admiring females happy, and he was impressed enough by what he heard from the nervous young man that he offered him a contract. But first he had to have a change of name — at Ted's suggestion, of course. And so Dickie Bryce became Dickie Valentine.

Towards the end of the year a letter and a photograph landed on Ted's desk from a Liverpool girl who was, at that time, living in America. She was in this country on holiday and feeling very homesick; also her marriage to an American soldier had not turned out very well. She'd heard the band, considered it to be the best, and wrote and asked Ted if if she could join him, enclosing a recording of her singing. Ted liked the look of Lita Roza (who wouldn't!) and her record confirmed that she was a singer of some talent. Lita joined the band early in 1950 and stayed for 4½ years.

With the acquisition of a couple of new singers Ted's bid to capture a wider audience was now beginning to take shape. But slowly, and

There was a danger in Ted's thoughts that certain players would be impossible to replace

almost disastrously. At the time of a 4-week variety tour of the Empire theatres at Chiswick, Hackney, Wood Green and Shepherd's Bush, Ted knew that the patrons of music halls belonged to a different age group from the majority of the band's followers, and that it would have been useless facing them with normal concert material. Swing was out, and the new Heath commercial approach was in.

However, Ted was soon to find out that there was a heavy price to pay for this transition. The band's regular fans threw their arms up in horror by what they regarded as something bordering on treachery. The change in the band's material was totally unacceptable to them. Ted also suffered in another way, too. His musicians — those who had considered his outfit to be a "musician's band" — were not too happy either about the change of direction.

That great trumpet player Kenny Baker left and so, too, did drumming favourite Jack Parnell, who decided to try his luck by forming his own outfit in 1951. There was a danger in Ted's thoughts that players like these would be almost impossible to replace, but the band still enjoyed a very high reputation among musicians of this country and Ted found highly competent replacements.

With his two new vocalists Ted was quite satisfied with the performances of Dickie Valentine and Lita Roza. Both, in their own ways, proved to be satisfactory and led almost proportionately as crowd-pleasing elements. It was at this juncture, when the fans accepted the band and its singers, that Ted received a visitor from South Africa at his office.

He was another singer, but Ted wasn't quite sure at that time that he needed another one. However, in view of the fact that Dennis Lotis was married and had children, and had sold his home to raise the fare to England in order to try his luck, Ted felt duty-bound to hear him sing — it was the least that he could do.

Dennis was nervous, but not in the same way that Dickie had been. The main difference between the two was that Dennis possessed a whole lot of assurance. Realising that Paul Carpenter couldn't stay with him forever, Ted decided that Dennis might very well be the person to step into Paul's shoes, and so he gave him a chance. Dennis, needless to say, grabbed at it with both hands, but it was a couple of years, however, before he really endeared himself to the fans.

Ted persevered with him until his faith in him was justified. But when Paul departed Ted changed his plans, and instead of Dennis taking on the compere's role he decided to do the job himself — after all, up to this point he had become known as the man of very few words.

In the autumn of 1952 Ted reached the summit of his own particular hill for the very first time since the band was formed: his bank account

50

showed a credit balance. To a great extent this was due to sales of the band's records, not merely in the matter of royalties, but in other ways, too. A hit record for someone like Ted's band not only sold well, but it also had a knock-on effect. The public wanted more records, and it also wanted to see more and more of the band in the flesh. As the saying goes, nothing succeeds like success.

Back in the summer of 1951 Lita's version of "Allentown Jail", accompanied by Ted's band, had made a great impression and really helped to establish her name as a singer. And in the following February an instrumental, "Hawaiian Mambo", had been seized upon by a hungry record-buying public. Next came "Obsession", with a lively and dynamic score by Reg Owen, which was tailor-made for the swing fans, and the listeners of BBC's "Housewives Choice" and "Family Favourites".

Proudly, Ted found himself with another hit on his hands. Others followed and the vaults of public esteem had been cracked wide open. At long last Ted's band had won its struggle to reach the top, and with bookings into bigger halls at higher fees the only problem left was how to remain there.

When Ted Heath reflected on his life he was surprised at what riches (not necessarily money) came his way. His band was now at the top, and with being in such a lofty position along came the opportunity to travel with his beloved outfit of musicians and play in such places as Australia, New Zealand, Ireland, Norway, Sweden, Denmark, Germany, Holland, France, Israel, Egypt and, of course, the United States. Ted regarded this as one of the biggest advantages of musical fluency, and he believed that the dreariness of his early life — particularly his busking days in the streets of London's West End — developed in him the capacity to enjoy the benefits of his hard-earned success.

On the surface Ted looked to be a rather poker-faced person and lacking in humour, and because of this he was given a nickname by his former pianist, Frank Horrox, which is revealed in the final chapter. In fact, this was far from being the case for the man derived great pleasure from the small and somewhat simple things of life.

In the material world he placed the greatest emphasis on two things: his wrist watch and his car — and only then because of practical reasons. He was a very punctual man and he needed to know the correct time, at all times, in order to plan his very hectic programming and travelling arrangements, and his needs for a car were obvious considering the lack of public transport at the times when the band managed to get away from a venue.

He had no desire to own the biggest and shiniest car, and throughout his bandleading career there was always at least one member of his band who owned a more luxurious car than he did! Once again, this gives an insight into the kind of money that Ted was generously paying to his musicians.

There was also another side to the man that his adoring swing fans knew little or nothing about. He was not a person who saved and he had no desire to amass a great deal of money. And there was many an occasion when a promoter lost money through booking Ted's band; yet those same promoters were handed back part of the takings, by Ted himself, when perhaps bad weather might have been the cause for keeping the expected large crowds away.

Now on the surface that might sound to be bad business, and to large degree that's true. But Ted's philosophy was a genuine belief that one does not lose out by gestures of this kind. Bread cast upon the waters has a habit of finding its way back, he maintained. More than once he was proved to be right.

One example in particular was his visit to Australia in 1954. It arose after an Irish/Australian show business manager, Jack Neary, visited the Palladium for one of Ted's Sunday swing sessions. He was completely overwhelmed by what he saw and heard, and he was determined to present the Heath band in Australia at whatever the cost. Ted had reservations (despite Neary's positive sense of successful optimism) and he insisted on striking a hard financial bargain — not out of avarice, but more from a sense of self-preservation.

With another concert over, Ted and a group of his musicians relax in the lounge of their hotel. This gave them the chance to unwind and hold an inquest into the evening's performance, and to toss around ideas for future programmes. Discussions such as this would go on until the early hours, which sometimes proved too much for Johnnie Gray, on the right of the picture!

Swapping the baton for a bat! Ted takes the crease for a match against Blackpool Football Club in 1947. Sir Stanley Matthews plays an unaccustomary role as wicketkeeper, while Blackpool skipper Harry Johnston is ready to pounce on any slip that Ted makes.

Before that, however, a furore was caused as a result of an interview with a writer on one of America's musical magazines, Down-Beat, who misconstrued Ted's answers to his questions regarding the Stateside big-band scene. In fact, not only was he misconstrued, but he was also misquoted and, in the most relevant summing-up passages, was not even quoted at all.

Not unnaturally American dance band fans screamed their heads off both in protest and defence of their musical idols, and they labelled the innocent Englishman egotistical, conceited and above all big-headed. An article which subsequently followed up the outburst went on to describe Ted's band as being inferior in every department to a very ordinary US service band that just happened to be touring Britain at that particular time.

Both the sound and the fury dragged on for several weeks, and Ted received little support from any quarter. Fans and critics alike were convinced that he had spoken rashly and in misplaced confidence. Remember, that what Ted was alleged to have said was done so in the backyard of the likes of Basie, Kenton and Ellington, and so he was deemed by many to have committed something approaching the treachery of a cardinal sin.

The whole affair hurt Ted's pride; enthusiasts could be forgiven for their scorn because everyone is entitled to his own opinion. In Ted's case, as a knowledgeable observer, he understood in great detail the complexities of the American band industry, and his opinion should have been accepted and examined with an open mind, and certainly not by the vitriol which had been whipped up by a trial in print that had been caused by certain sensation-seeking correspondents.

However, people have short memories, and within a short space of time the waters calmed, Ted's records began to sell in large numbers in America and the hard and indisputable fact of the success of Ted's band, on its tour over there, was to prove to be a vindication of his own opinions. In short, he was to be eventually forgiven by those whose hackles had been raised at the time.

But Ted was not to know this and he was in an extremely, yet at the same time excited frame of mind, as he and his musicians set sail on a history-making voyage across the Atlantic, aboard the Queen Mary, on March 22, 1956.

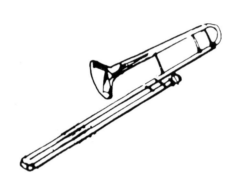

CHAPTER FIVE

Two-Way Visits Across the Atlantic

 One of the most important factors in the history of the band was that the compliments which Ted and his men received came not only from this country but also from America — the undoubted home of swing music which Ted, via his recordings, was beginning to exploit in such a successful manner.

For a band — especially a British outfit — to be rated alongside the American big five was an achievement of astronomic and almost unbelievable proportions. But rated Ted was and unquestionably recognised by these same bandleaders as a member of their own elite league, and known as the contemporaries of swing.

With his records selling in vast numbers it therefore came as no surprise to learn that the US audiences wanted to see the Heath band for themselves, and to judge whether or not their own revered heroes of swing music were, perhaps, erring a little in their appraisal of "This Heath guy from England".

But there were complications on this issue. Although the British audiences admired the American outfits (and by some curious line of reasoning considered them to be far superior to our own) those same bands never played in Britain — except for their visits to the numerous USAF bases in various parts of the country — and the British bands were never allowed to tour the States.

The reason for this was because they were banned from doing so by their respective unions, and it was a ridiculous, red-tape situation which had been in existence since 1935.

You see, they even had union troubles in those days, too!

A success for the Duke on a second tour in the Fifties

Duke Ellington, one of the greatest big-band inspirations of all time, was one of the many American bandleaders who visited these shores on exchange visits after the Anglo-American musicians' union ban was lifted in the mid-Fifties.

On this occasion his visit was a success, and it saw him and his orchestra playing to packed venues everywhere he went — unlike the time in 1948 when he almost made history by playing to an audience of only 150.

The appreciative British crowds could see and hear for themselves many of the Duke's classic numbers, played in the style with which they were intended.

Can you imagine for a moment the situation of pure farce which was prevalent at the time of this acrimonious yet petty-fogging ban? Is it at all conceivable that bands of the calibre and status of Glenn Miller and Les Brown, to name just two, were only allowed to be here in this country for the sole purpose of entertaining the servicemen who were based at the United States Air Force camps, and yet not permitted to tour the country for the rest of us to see?

Inconceivable, maybe, but true it most certainly was.

And yet there was a half-way mark — a lifeline of compromise.

For example, an American bandleader on his own, and without his own musicians, was allowed to give concerts up and own the country provided that he was backed by British musicians. That was part of the acrimony of the ban.

The following incident of lunacy, caused by that ban, will give some idea as to what went on and how unsuccessful and inconsistent its enforcement proved to be. Once again it took place in Buxton, and at the very same venue where I first met Ted. However, this event occurred in 1948, which was five years earlier.

It seems hard to comprehend that there were many times in the illustrious career of Duke Ellington when this legendary man of jazz and swing played to anything less than a capacity audience — not even in times of war or financial hardship.

Naturally there must have been the odd auditorium, up and down the country, which found itself with one or two unsold seats on its hands. But they say that nothing is stranger than fact, so bear that adage in mind as you read on. For during a tour which the Duke made that year he visited Buxton . . . and attracted a crowd of no more than 150. Yes, 150!

Yet the night before this concert hundreds had queued for up to three hours, at one sold-out venue, merely in the hope of a cancellation and the chance to obtain tickets. Hooked? Then read on!

Saturday, July 17, 1948, will be well remembered by those who formed the queues outside the Hammersmith Palais in London and who then packed the place to hear Ellington. For those who had waited patiently for hours, and were then unable to obtain tickets for this concert, it was nothing short of a let-down and a bitter disappointment.

But what a different story it was the next day when Ellington travelled north to Buxton, to a venue which had, over the years, developed and enjoyed an excellent reputation as a dancer's mecca.

From a rather parochial book which I wrote in the Seventies, and titled "The Big Band Era of Buxton", I quote the following paragraphs:

"To say that the concert was a success would be a gross overstatement, for with seating arrangements for 1,000 people only 150 turned up to listen to the jazz giant from across the Atlantic.

"One can only surmise that the management of the day must have been frustrated to say the least, not to mention the promoter Harold Fielding, that such a low turnout was experienced. Was it possibly a cross between ignorance and disinterest? No one will ever know".

As an afterthought to the frustrations of the management, and Harold Fielding, it is indeed debateable just how Ellington himself must have felt about the turnout. No doubt he must have had many reservations, and some doubts, as to whether or not he had turned up at the right venue!

Not unnaturally, perhaps, the town's local newspaper, the Buxton Advertiser, when it reviewed the book, either took me to task over my criticism of the poor attendance or it tried to do a cover-up job by saying that news of the appearance of Duke Ellington had not been circulated well enough.

The newspaper's critic wrote: "The event was arranged only a short time before it took place, and the advertising opportunities were therefore very limited. Mr Ellington did comment on the small audience, but he trusted that what it lacked in attendance figures it made up for in interest and appreciation of jazz"

The personnel consisted of Ellington being backed by Britain's Jack Fallon Trio with Fallon on bass, Malcolm Mitchell on guitar and drummer Tony Crombie. Also featured on the bill that Sunday afternoon were singers Ray Nance and Kay Davis.

But if there was an acute shortage of musicians (as well as patrons) then this was amply compensated for by the quality of the musical programme. For as long ago as 1948 the Ellington numbers, which we know so well and love to hear so much, had been written. And even by the standards of that particular period they were well and truly on the way to becoming the classics they are now.

"Caravan", "Solitude", "Sophisticated Lady", "Take the A Train" and "In a Sentimental Mood" were all included in a programme played for such a paltry audience, but which made the event musically viable, if not financially profitable.

To a professional other than Ellington that concert would, to use the appropriate show-business adjective, have 'killed' him; it most certainly would have done to a lesser-known mortal. But an eye-witness (during my research I actually found one of the 150 who attended that concert) said that the Duke never faltered.

"What a show it was," he said. "At the end everyone present gave him a standing ovation, and I'm sure that in his heart he realised that although he'd played to such a small number those who had attended really appreciated his music."

It is one of those rare and strange — sometimes inexplicable — symptoms of life that the Pavilion Gardens in Buxton was definitely NOT a good concert venue. And yet, during the Fifties, the place enjoyed the reputation of being one of the top dance venues in the country, attracting every 'name' band in the country. And I do mean EVERY band.

Musical history can, of course, be made at any time, and it isn't just confined to a six months prior sell-out concert at somewhere like New York's Carnegie Hall in order to make it. It can be made in a sleepy English town, 1,000 feet above sea level, on a quiet Sunday afternoon.

I suspect Duke Ellington made history on that day in July, 1948; or was it the absent crowds who made it? The answer is arguable.

What a difference, no doubt, the atmosphere was the night before at the Hammersmith Palais. The ironic thing here is that Hammersmith, too, had a dancers' reputation as a top mecca but, unlike Buxton, it proved that it could successfully stage a concert — especially one of such value and importance.

Ted made no secret of the fact that he desperately wanted to take his band to America and, thanks to the behind-the-scenes negotiations which involved Stan Kenton, the unions, Tutti Camarata and Ted himself, he was rewarded with his desire when the agreement called for a Kenton-Heath exchange.

But its recognition as the best band in Britain helped to promote the American Federation of Musicians and the English Musicians' Union to join forces, sit around the table, pull down the bureaucratic barriers and patch up their past differences and grievances. This they did, and a reciprocal agreement was worked out in 1956.

And so Stan arrived in Britain to kick off the much-talked-about and long-awaited tour in London and, it was hoped, to lay the ghost of the musicians' union ban once and for all.

60

***Stan Kenton, who along with Ted, Carlos Gastele and Tutti Camarata, helped
to break down the musicians' unions ban which had been in force since 1935.***

Ted took his band to the States as part of a package which included Nat King Cole and the Four Freshmen, and perhaps not unnaturally had the American audiences eating out of the palm of his hand. In a later chapter Ronnie Verrell describes just how successful the visit really was.

Ted had the American audiences eating out of the palm of his hand

At the packed and now-demolished King's Hall at Belle Vue, Manchester, I sat, watched and listened as Stan Kenton, America's greatest and — as far as swing fans in this country were concerned — most popular exponent of big-band rhythms thrilled the crowd with his noted brassy sound by almost lifting the roof and, at the same time, possibly registering 5 points on the Richter scale!

Loud and shattering, as his sound most certainly was, this indeed was Kenton at his very best. And, as at venues prior to Manchester, the enthusiasm of his audience proved that he could no wrong.

With progressive arrangements and compositions such as "Peanut Vendor", "Artistry in Rhythm", "Intermission Riff" and "Concerto to End All Concertos", played as only Kenton could, there was no doubting the popularity of the man nor the unswerving gratitude that the notorious musicians' ban had been lifted.

Here at last was the living, musical legend in the flesh. Trying to be neutral (and I do stress the word trying, because I wanted to be a member of that crowd as much as anyone else) I sat there and asked myself: "So this is Kenton!" Dominant, positive, decisive — brash even. But above all impressive, and good. Very good.

There on the stage of the 6,000-seater King's Hall, with a capacity audience enthralled by the best of his kind in America, set me thinking. If this was the British reaction to Stan Kenton, then what would the US audiences make of our premier band? How would they rate Ted Heath?

Stan had instrumentalists of the calibre of Vinnie Tanno, Bill Perkins and Curtis Counce in his line-up to add all the necessary star clout. But then Ted didn't exactly go to the US empty handed. How could he when he went totally equipped with musicians like Don Lusher, Bobby Pratt, Ronnie Verrell and Johnny Hawksworth?

The Kenton sound must have registered about 5 points on the Richter scale!

No, it was a case of anything Kenton could do, Ted Heath could do as well — if not better. And this wasn't just confined to his star musicians either. Don't forget, when the time came for Ted to take his band to the States he, too, had a whole string of numbers tucked under his belt ready to deliver to his audiences over there.

Britain's record-buying public had firmly made Ted's band its number one by putting records such as "Hot Toddy", "The Faithful Hussar", "Swinging Shepherd Blues" and "Cloudburst" in the record charts which, in the Fifties, were still very much in their infancy.

By the time Kenton's tour had ended the British audiences were hungry for more visits by the US bands, and the second exchange involved Britain's Freddie Randall crossing the Atlantic allowing Louis Armstrong's All Stars to visit this country.

Somehow it doesn't seem like 37 years since I paid the almost ransom-like sum of 30/- (£1.50) for a ringside seat at the Liverpool Stadium for Armstrong's concert in May, 1956.

It was of course only natural that personnel changes, as far as the first-half accompanists went, were inevitable, and while the Vic Lewis Orchestra played with Louis at most of the venues on his British tour, a little home-spun philosophy was applied when he visited Liverpool with the Merseysippi Jazz Band (what a marvellous name) taking the first-half rostrum.

There are those who might argue that a warm May evening can be spent doing other things than sitting in a boxing arena listening to jazz: this was borne out by the vast number of empty seats, and the attendants moving everyone forward from the rear in order that a better appreciation might be felt.

It certainly made me wonder whether I'd been a bit extravagant at paying thirty bob when those in the 7/6's got just as good a seat!

The revolving rostrum at the stadium did nothing but help, and although the arena was recognised as anything but a concert venue the accoustics for such an event were greatly amplified by the centrepiece, and not in the least bit distractive.

The only drawback at staging a concert like this was the impossibility of being able to introduce the band in any other way than the almost undignified approach to the stage via the aisles. Louis and his men walked down to the platform rather like a boxer and his entourage.

But casting aside this anomaly Louis lived up to all the newspaper reports that he went through 92 white handkerchiefs during each performance. On this count I couldn't argue, for I actually lost count after 50!

You may recall that at the time of Armstrong's visit he and his band were hit parade celebrities by virtue of their best-selling records "Mack the Knife" and "The Faithful Hussar". It was, probably, the first major step by Louis towards establishing himself as a commercial entity — a recording force who no longer had to rely solely on the elements of jazz to radiate his already envious personality.

As with the demands on their football teams the Liverpool crowd had gone along to see and hear the best, and Louis duly obliged. All the tricks of his particular trade he put on display: the rolling eyes, the humour (of which Scousers know a bit) and of course that legendary voice which was once described as "A mixture of nuts, bolts, iron filings and stones all thrown into a tin can containing a liberal amount of engine oil, and rattled."

For sheer entertainment value, and thoroughbred professionalism, the Liverpool concert by Armstrong and his All Stars was a unique and unforgettable experience. And at 30/- it was also a lesson, on my part, in sheer economics!

In 1957 another US legend arrived. Count Basie brought his orchestra to Britain for the first time ever, in exchange for the Vic Lewis Orchestra. The Basie aggregation had long been widely known in Britain since the Thirties, with its output of precision-packed and swinging recordings of a consistently high standard. The Count's arrival could not possibly have come at a more appropriate time, for he was riding high over here with his "April in Paris" recording.

Basie's audiences rose to every performance. In addition to the orchestra's impeccable ensemble, especially the saxophone section, there was the driving and almost frantic drumming of Sonny Payne, which seemed to lose nothing as the result of his persistent juggling with his drum sticks.

At the concert I attended, at the City Hall in Sheffield, there was one thing passing through my mind as the sticks seemed to be as much in the air as they were in Sonny's hands: what if they suddenly went elsewhere and ended up other than where they should be? Thankfully, Sonny left the question in abeyance; the worst never happened.

But what impressed me most about Basie, apart from his ease at handling the meticulous and seemingly-difficult musical arrangements, was his no-gimmicks approach to leadership, no prancing about, no toothy grins and no unnecessary arm waving. A true professional in every sense of the word, and underscoring his standing and authority over one of the world's greatest swing bands.

It must have been with a certain amount of trepidation that Duke Ellington revisited Britain in 1958, especially after his ill-fated trip 10 years earlier. But this time things were very different. This time he had the natural support of his own orchestra and when I saw him, once again at the Belle Vue, Manchester, venue, the full-house attendance made a mockery of his 1948 nightmare visit, and truly vindicated the wisdom of scrapping that now-notorious ban. In short, the Duke couldn't put a foot wrong.

Although the Ellington outfit was one of the greatest, there were many who had switched their loyalties to the Basie orchestra; the Count, however, was always the first to dispute any suggestion that his was the superior ensemble. This was in no sense a case of false modesty, either, but a genuine respect for a great musician who had for several decades modelled a magnificent band, and assembled a 100 per cent catalogue of self-penned standards.

Another interesting exchange took place in 1958, and this involved one of Ted's former and original band members from the 1945 period — tenor saxist Johnnie Gray, who crossed the Atlantic in exchange for Norman Granz's Jazz at the Philharmonic package. This was something of a curiosity deal really, for Johnnie with his Band of the Day bore no resemblance whatsoever in style to that of the JATP.

After being in Ted's employ — in fact, even while he was still in it — Johnnie developed a spicy style of solo work, and also became involved in comedy presentation. With his boisterous personality and enormous moustache being an integral part of his stock-in-trade, Johnnie eventually went solo in cabaret and in the clubs which were springing to life on a regular basis in the late Fifties and early Sixties.

So there must be many younger musicians around today who, although they've heard the name of course, cannot possibly remember Johnnie as a member of Ted's early and formidable reed section, which included players such as Les Gilbert, Reg Owen, Ronnie Scott, Dave Shand and Tommy Whittle.

But don't worry, fellas, neither can I!

Before dispensing with the passage on Ellington, however, there is a story regarding the Duke's former singer Al Hibbler, who was backed by Ted on one of his tours of the States.

Al Hibbler's singing style was distinctly recognisable by his deep, rich tones and crystal-clear diction — a facet which was a teaser and belied the fact that he was coloured. His universal success with "Unchained Melody", and the demand for his services, meant that his British fans had to join the queue before he eventually toured this country.

Meanwhile Hibbler, the unlikeliest of hit parade singers, notched up two more very creditable hits with "He" and "The Eleventh Hour Melody". The time was now apparently ripe for Al to tour Britain. However, as with a number of other aspects of showbusiness, there are still a great number of artists who rely heavily on the somewhat and sometimes debased voice of the critic — wrong as they very often can be. And there was no doubt that Al Hibbler suffered at the hands of the critics in general, and one rather unsavoury colleague in particular.

I have very good reasons for not naming the journalist concerned, nor the musical paper for which he worked — not the least of which is expediency. In the first place I always used to have the greatest respect for the newspaper, but as for the critic, well, the least said about him the better.

But to give you some idea as to his criticism of Hibbler (and remember the singer was blind and had to be led on to the stage to the microphone) this obviously misplaced hack wrote: "Al Hibbler stands and delivers his songs in the most pedestrian way by just standing there at the microphone. If only he would move about a bit."

Just how callous can a reviewer get? What did he expect from a blind man? Did he register some sort of shock, horror, surprise because Hibbler didn't suddenly break out into a song and dance routine? I hope that critic reads this with a heavy mixture of embarrassment on the one hand and relief on the other that he hasn't been named. As a footnote, Al Hibbler had no more hits nor did he visit these shores again.

65

In coming to this country when he did, in 1956, Lionel Hampton couldn't have chosen a worse time if he'd tried. Britain, like America, was in the grip of rock n' roll, which consequently saw a disturbingly-high number of the big bands going to the wall.

But it wasn't only the timing of the tour that was ill-arranged, but a lot to do with the material which he played.

Unfortunate as it was, there were a number of the rock groups and singers who chose to play numbers which were associated with Hamp, and they recorded them.

Consequently it was then that Hamp found himself in a Catch-22 situation, because when he began to play those numbers (just as he had been doing for years) he was accused by the critics of jumping on the wagon and playing rock music.

Lionel Hampton's performances suffered at the hands of the critics — even though it was through no fault of his own. His resilience, however, won through in the end, but not until after a somewhat surprising taunt from one particular member of his audience.

Numbers like "Midnight Sun" had been given the rock treatment by others, and bore no resemblance to the way that Hamp had played it in the past. And when "Shake, Rattle and Roll" (another number long associated with Hampton) was hammered out by his band it only added fuel to the slowly-burning fire. What made things worse was that he played it with a 2-4 beat, and any number which was given this kind of treatment was automatically labelled rock n' roll.

Poor old Hamp — he really was in a no-win situation.

Of course by wearing a rather brash and shiny purple stage suit he didn't exactly do much to help to dampen down the unwanted image of a middle-aged rocker, or indeed endear himself to those who had been swayed by the newspaper reviews. On his tour of the country he certainly played to some exciting audiences, but he also had his critics, too.

"Some guys who wrote for Melody Maker, the big British musical newspaper, started complaining in print that we weren't playing enough jazz. I didn't pay much attention, because *I* knew what I was playing," said Hamp.

It wasn't until a concert at London's Royal Festival Hall that the truth of the situation dawned on Hamp when a voice, reputed to be that of Johnny Dankworth, shouted out: "Why don't you play some jazz?"

A lot of British musicians were embarrassed by Dankworth's outburst, and 33 of them sent a letter to the Melody Maker stating:

> *"As British musicians, representative of many schools, we wish to dissociate ourselves from Johnny Dankworth's views and actions, and from the severe criticisms of Hampton's shows which have been aired by the Melody Maker.*
>
> *"Whether at the Festival Hall, or on other occasions, we heartily enjoyed the show — full of jazz content — put on by this swinging band. And we are prepared to accept and enjoy supreme artists like Lionel Hampton and Louis Armstrong on their terms."*

But from a business point of view all this controversy came in extremely useful, for Hamp became a front-page item and that meant it was good for the box office. After reading about the incident a lot of people, who might otherwise have not gone to one of his concerts, decided that they wanted to see for themselves what all the fuss was about.

When Ted visited America the first time his records over there were issued on the London label, as opposed to his releases over here being put out by Decca. The London label in the States was started and run by Tutti Camarata, who proved to be a marvellous friend to Ted and someone who, consequently, this country proved to be indebted to as a result of his efforts in opening the doors for not only Ted, but also for Vera Lynn, Mantovani and Frank Chacksfield.

But just as Hamp had suffered, for different reasons, in this country so, too, did Ted at one particular concert in which he was backing Nat King Cole in Birmingham, Alabama, and which almost resulted in him throwing in the towel and bringing his band back home, after Nat was attacked on stage. The concert in question was played before a segregated audience, with blacks on one side of the auditorium and whites on the other.

Prior to the concert it had been arranged that Ted's band would play behind a screen so that it couldn't be seen — even the performers had to be segregated. Nat had already sung two numbers and all was going well when, according to a Time magazine report, all hell broke loose and 5 men ran down the aisles and bounded on to the stage.

Audience trouble, during a US concert tour with Nat King Cole, turned out to be anything but a bed of roses with Ted seriously considering cancelling the rest of the tour and bringing his musicians home

Ted pictured with Nat King Cole, when the pair toured the States as part of the same musical package.

One hit Nat and sent him staggering, causing him to fall backwards over the piano stool and sustaining a split lip. The police rushed in and the musicians, who were now beginning to feel physically sick, helped them to rescue Nat. Needless to say that particular concert came to an abrupt and frightening ending.

Ted was not in the concert hall that night when the incident took place, but he took a lot of persuading to stay — especially when the story was flashed on to television news broadcasts across America, and not long after appeared in all of the British newspapers.

But despite Ted being very proud of his musicians in helping to quell the dangerous situation, he got hold of Carlos Carruthers, Nat's manager, and told him that he'd rather call the whole thing off and take his men home, rather than endure another such horrible experience. But Ted did fulfil the tour, which culminated in a never-to-be-forgotten Carnegie Hall concert in New York.

● One amusing tableau springs to the mind of Ken Kiddier with regards to that first, memorable trip to the States, when Ted's band accompanied the Four Freshmen, June Christy and Al Hibbler.

"We had stopped to refuel in the middle of an overnight trip," recalls Ken. "The tanks of the Greyhound coach held around 250 gallons, which took about 20 minutes to fill, and we'd all trooped into the ever-present Howard Johnson diner for a coffee or whatever.

68

"Gathering outside afterwards, at the pre-determined time, we shiveringly awaited the replenished coach. It hove into view weaving its way through the parking lot to halt exactly opposite the bunch of weary travellers. The driver leaned from his window, removed his cap and, in a very passable Bela Lugosi voice, observed: 'Room for one more inside, gentlemen'.

"It was Al Hibbler — blind from birth — being guided by the real driver who was crouched in the seat behind. We fell about with laughter, for it was little gems like that which stick in the mind.

When Al was singer with Ellington, and the focus of many radio interviews, the interviewer would invariably bring up the emotive hardships of being blind. And Al was always quite adamant that it was he who first coined that famous quote: 'It's better than being born black'."

With the triumphs of the American visits tucked beneath his belt and his reputation world-wide rapidly gaining momentum, Ted Heath was now in a very strong position, first to make the music critics sit up on their haunches and second to give them cause to eat their words over his criticisms of the Stateside band industry. His interview with Down Beat had subsequently been picked up by the musical press in this country, and now that he was back home Ted earnestly set about the task of redressing the biased balance.

To the editors he wrote: *"I realise that you have a job to do, as I have, and that some times puts us at cross-purposes. I know that I go off at the deep end if I don't agree with what you've written, but often, after I've cooled down, I admit that you might be right. But not always."*

The Down Beat interview was one that Ted found extremely hard to swallow. In his mind a savage attack on a British band (just because its leader had dared to say that all American bands didn't live up to the high reputation that they enjoyed in this country) smacked of treachery. Patriotism should not have affected the issue, for some British musicians enjoyed a higher reputation in the States than they did in this country; they had to be judged on performance. And vice versa.

Ted's argument was that although the very best US bands were indeed formidable, it didn't automatically mean that *every* band was superior to *any* British outfit. Indeed, no knowledgeable American would make such a claim — and Ted said so. But his comments to the interviewer fell on deaf ears, and it was these omissions from the finished copy which caused the furore. But Ted's performances in America had silenced his critics, and a large number of the band's recordings had been given rave notices — which was all extra power to his elbow.

With all of this in mind there was one very important and contributory factor which, in spite of all the previous aggravation, was in Ted's favour; it was that his band did not have a fabulous reputation to live up to. In that respect he had a very distinct and perhaps a psychological edge on Stan Kenton, whose band was to tour in the exchange agreement, thanks to the lifting of the ban by the respective musicians' unions.

Stan had a great following over here, and only superlatives could justify the high expectations at the news of his visit. Not unnaturally, Ted wondered what might be said if his band failed or flopped in the States — not that he actually believed it would, of course. He lived, breathed and dreamed the band and was more than familiar with all its great strengths, as well as its very limited weaknesses. He also knew that its greatest asset was its versatility. Prior to departing Ted told himself that the Americans couldn't, in all honesty, say that he had a bad band.

Well, those lingering doubts of his steamed away as soon as "Kings Cross Climax" pulled out of Carnegie Hall and began its journey along the rails of America, pulling in at the many stations on the gruelling tour from the east to west coasts. It left Ted almost in tears as he and his musicians soaked up the tremendous ovations which they received. On occasions such as this — and probably for the first time in his career — he was rendered speechless, but he managed to hide his feelings by turning to his men and allowing them to cover for him and take the full force of the enthusiastic fans' acknowledgements.

Had Ted Heath been alive today he would have been 93. But even as far back as 1957, when he was 57 years old, he was asked on many occasions when he intended to retire. Ted's answer to this rather pointed question was: "When I see the writing on the wall, and when I realise that I can't stay at the top." This was a very positive and perceptive reply, for Ted now knew that his beloved dream band was in just such a spot — at the very top.

Even so, he was conscious of his greying hair and the belief that the dance band business was a young man's occupation. But there was more to Ted's answer than any of the questioners could possibly have realised at the time of asking. He was quite sincere of course in his reply, but having reached the pinnacle he could not bear the thought of ever being second-best. That was the real crux of his answer.

Ted had good reason for this particular line of thinking, even though at the time many of the less-informed would have thought that he was becoming a little paranoid. But the truth was that other British bands were nudging at him all the time — many of them led by just such younger men. One such leader, Johnny Dankworth, paid him the highest compliment one day in the course of a conversation. "Ted, wouldn't I like to ask you a hundred questions on running a band successfully!"

Ted regarded Johnny, Jack Parnell and others as his friends, and he was prepared to give them full credit for what they had achieved to date. But, more important, he could never lose sight that they were his competitors. Consequently, he assured them that they would have to work 'mighty hard' to dislodge the Ted Heath band from the lofty pinnacle on which it stood.

Again, this was said with good reason for the visits to America gave every one of his musicians an almighty shot of increased confidence in their own capabilities, and the band was playing better than it had ever done before. But is was at this juncture that a cruel twist of fate occurred in the notoriously-fickle music industry.

Times were changing; tastes were changing and so, too, were the musical vogues. Traditional and New Orleans jazz was beginning to enjoy a revival in this country (naturally being a knock-on effect from the States) and in doing so it was pushing big-band music further towards the back of the musical queue. As did rock and roll.

Ted held neither in very high esteem, and refused point-blank to even consider compromising the reputation of his band by playing any part in this new wave of musical appeal. In fact Ted's view of it all was that the Trads tapped the same undiscerning audience as the lusty rock idiom. But he claimed that the rockers and rollers were more honest because they didn't claim that theirs was an art form. Consequently a very large proportion of the record-buying public were young, and the expenditure on what was termed 'popular music' was enormous, and rose rapidly.

By any stretch of the imagination, and probably against all the odds, Ted was able to survive — albeit not as easy as before. With the changing trends came the variation of band formations. Rapidly disappearing were the familiar and homely 16-piece line-ups of five saxes, four trombones, four trumpets and rhythm sections. It was now a time of guitars, three-chord wonders, tea-chest basses and even washboards, which hammered out anything which could be remotely handled up-tempo. In economic terms it was no contest: a five-man combo came at a third of the price (or less) than a 16-piece band, and dance and swing music was well and truly on its way out of the window.

Despite all this, however, Ted wasn't doing too badly in terms of record sales. His discs were there sharing the hit parade alongside the likes of Bill Haley, Elvis Presley, Jerry Lee Lewis, Fats Domino and all the others who helped to break the mould in musical trends. Yet against this backdrop of gold-record winners, the loyal fans of the Heath band made sure that the rockers, the skifflers and the rest didn't have things all their own way. They also proved that Ted was still very much in demand by snapping up his recordings.

"The Creep", "Swinging Shepherd Blues", "The Faithful Hussar", "Hot Toddy", "Tom Hark" and "Cloudburst" all kept the wolf from the door, and the band on the road. This was quite an achievement for other aggregations were falling by the wayside and disbanding, with some of the musicians from those bands chancing their arms by attempting to cash in (in some small degree) on the new idioms. It has to be said that only a minor number were successful, and even then not for long.

But the paramount query all along the line at this time was how much longer could the Ted Heath band stay at the top? The question was soon to be answered in very saddening circumstances.

Touring with a band half way across the world and back again, together with all the responsibilities which the job as leader entails, is bound to take its toll on the health of the strongest of individuals — especially if those tours are, for the most part, one-night stands. Ted was no exception to the rule. In the early 1960s almost 20 years of non-stop touring eventually caught up with him. The result of the pressures and strains of creating his dream band, taking it to the very top and keeping it there proved too much, and a breakdown followed. Perhaps too soon he returned to the bandstand to continue with his arduous schedule — with his fans and followers knowing little or nothing of his health condition.

But even after his return to lead the band, it became obvious to those who were closest to him (his family and his musicians) that all was not right. Finally, in the late Sixties, it all proved too much and Ted's health failed him yet again. This time it was permanent.

He was forced to enter a nursing home where both his physical and mental condition tragically continued to deteriorate. His death in November, 1969, was to prove to be the ending of an era the likes of which the big-band world had never before seen. His demise left a void which has never been filled and, with all due respect to bandleaders everywhere, never will be.

Ted Heath was unique — a one-off — and he left behind a musical legacy for the world to enjoy for all time.

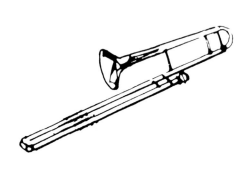

CHAPTER SIX

The Bands of Revivalists

 In some parts of the country there is more than a passing buzz that the big bands are on the way back and long overdue for a revival, while in other parts, however, there is the argument that they've never been away! Of course big-band revivals are always being mooted, and have been ever since the bands nearly all faded away beneath the onslaught of rock n' roll in the Fifties, and all the other subsequent fads.

In 1955 when rock n' roll swept the shores of this country from America, many of the 'name' bands of the day were quick to jump on the wagon and play the new musical craze, big-band style. Ted Heath was one of the very few who survived because of his reputation and status, and because he never succombed to the temptation to follow the rest of the pack. He didn't need to for his music was his ideal, and his ideals were his principles.

Even though it was Jack Parnell and an all-star orchestra who was responsible for a big-band revival attempt in 1975, it was, however, veteran saxophonist Harry Bence, the leader of the New Squadronaires, who unashamedly laid the credit at the door of a bad-mannered and best-forgotten pop group called the Bay City Rollers.

The man who had played with the bands of Joe Loss, Ted and Geraldo had no hesitation, and added wryly: "We owe it all to the Rollers. They have made everyone — except the weeny-boppers — yearn again for good music, and they're turning back the clock to the pre-rock era of the Forties to find it. We ought to give that group a medal really!"

So just what was it that prompted the wily Harry Bence to rush into print in the Daily Mail with such enthusiasm?

It was his own personal reaction to the success of a marvellous one-hour show which had suddenly burst on to our television screens, almost without warning and at a peak-viewing time that night in September, 1975. And right from the first few bars it was obvious that "The Jack Parnell Big Band Show" was a hit. Of that there was no doubt.

Quite rightly the television company which made the programme, the now-defunct ATV, sat back and enjoyed many plaudits. After the show the ITV switchboards were jammed with calls of congratulations, so much so that ATV lost no time at all in getting another such show planned and into the pipeline.

That particular show was transmitted again at a peak-viewing time over the Christmas period, and once more the response proved that ATV had not erred in its decision to put out another programme of sheer musical and big-band nostalgia. Not unnaturally heads were put together at the company's Borehamwood headquarters in Hertfordshire, and the wheels were set in motion to produce a series.

What had started out as an accident proved to be the backbone of two very successful shows, and produced the format for a series of programmes which suddenly brought the music, and the original arrangements, of such stalwarts as Tommy Dorsey, Glenn Miller, Woody Herman, Count Basie, Duke Ellington and, of course, Ted Heath, back to life with a very positive bang.

The aforementioned 'accident' had occurred earlier in the year at, of all places, the London Palladium, when Jack's band was providing the backing for Caterina Valente and had to do a 45-minute slot on its own, before Caterina came on in the second half of the show.

Jack, a man never usually stumped for an idea, suddenly decided to use the original arrangements and he kept his fingers crossed in the hope that he had made the right decision. Jack slept very well that night, thank you! It went down so well with the Palladium audience that ATV offered him a one-off show to see if it would make good television. It did.

For that initial programme Jack was given a free hand to select his own musicians, and he lost no time at all in surrounding himself with the very best around. He could do no better than to choose his ex-Heath colleagues. Don Lusher, Kenny Baker, Ronnie Verrell, Bert Ezzard, Tommy Whittle, Lennie Bush and Norman Stenfalt were all lined up for that one-night stand which was to take viewers back on a nostalgic, musical trip and at the same time hopefully pick up a few young, uninitiated travellers along the way.

Bryan Blackburn scripted the show and all will have noticed that Jack, in his selection, played safer than safe. Perhaps he had a tendency to be just that wee bit biased — but who could blame him in all honesty? After all, it was his choice and he did want the best. The main thing is it worked; with players of that calibre how could it possibly have been any other way? But what about the series?

Sad to relate this proved to be one of the biggest cock-ups of all time — possibly in the history of television. And that's putting it mildly. The series didn't work, and one actually wonders if indeed it was ever meant to.

Now this might sound a little strange but we have all, on so many occasions, witnessed some of the most unusual of goings-on as far as the ITV network is concerned. You'll know what I mean when I say that if some of the programmes, which are shown at peak-viewing time, were taken apart and analysed for what they are they would amount to virtually nothing at all.

In other words, what is sometimes transmitted to us by the companies as family entertainment (their interpretation, not mine) is nothing short of being rubbish; in reality these programmes should never have been allocated a regional slot let alone a networked one.

All sorts of arguments arise here with the most powerful being the question as to whether a pilot — or one-off — should be made and transmitted to test the market before splashing out on a full-blown series.

This makes sense, for if a pilot show hasn't enough strength to lift it from the ground, then a series would never take off. So a lot of precious money can be saved — an admirable policy which the BBC has always stuck with, and pretty safely, too.

If a pilot does receive the hoped-for viewer reactions then the television company concerned can, justifiably, go about its business of producing a series. However, all is not plain sailing yet — if at all.

A deep-in-thought Jack, perhaps wondering why the politics of television scheduling were allowed to come before his successful show.

Once the series has been made it is usually stuck away on a shelf somewhere until the ITV schedules are decided upon. This, as one can imagine, is more difficult than it sounds for it is not just a question of selecting programmes for the network, but for the regions also.

And if you can try to visualise all the regional companies jockeying with each other to place one of its programmes on to the ITV network schedules, then you will also understand the in-fighting which is almost inevitable.

But most of this usually occurs over the promotion of some new and untried programme, and certainly not one that has already been accepted and proved to be a winner. All of which made "The Jack Parnell Big Band Show" something of an unaccountable embarrassment to ITV, rather than it being a jewel in its crown.

For when the programme planners had finished, and the schedules drawn up, the JPBBS found itself in a kind of no-man's land. Gone was its much-coveted, peak-time slot, and it was here that we found probably the biggest example of ITV planning gone wrong.

In many areas the series was not shown until after 10.30 pm — and even later than that in some places. Some regions never even saw it at all. So it's fair comment to observe that with many viewers, notably the younger ones, the programme was virtually doomed from the word go. After all, what chance did it possibly stand with those who had perhaps endured four or five hours viewing prior to Jack's programme coming on?

To these people (and they were bound to be tired and feeling square-eyed by then) and thousands of others the show had been reduced to nothing more than a filler — something to pad out the schedules with until bedtime. What a monumentally ludicrous situation for a hit musical series to find itself in!

In fairness to the BBC, its contribution to the television band scene at that time, "Band Beat", did at least go out at a respectable hour of the evening and it, like the two previous Parnell shows, caught the imagination of an attentive audience simply because there was an audience. Period.

As far as the JPBBS series content was concerned, and the quality, well that issue was never at stake. Indeed, with the musicians which formed Jack's band how could there possibly have been any arguments?

Bryan Blackburn, who was once again commissioned to write the scripts, had to be complimented on his meanness of words. Any lengthy chat and the series would have suffered an additional indignity; it had suffered not only being relegated to the late hour, but a further dose of salt was rubbed into the wound by a half-hour chop as well — so reducing it from one hour to 30 minutes.

What certainly didn't suffer were the musical arrangements; ethereal, professional (as you would imagine) and clinically delivered. But I must admit that I was not at all impressed with a studio arrangement which saw the brass section more than totally divorced from the reeds. It was only the brilliance and extra work of the rhythm section — Ronnie Verrell, Lennie Bush, Norman Stenfalt and Martin Kershaw — which bridged such an unnecessary gap.

Well, despite the lateness of the hour, the series came to an end. It was to be hoped that with the wisdom of hindsight the aforementioned problems could be ironed out before the start of the next series.

After all, there was going to another series . . . wasn't there?

Surely producer Alan Tarrant and Jack himself, as ATV's musical director, could lend their combined weight to ensure a better deal from ITV the next time around.

But with ITV anything can happen — and it usually does. The sad truth is that there wasn't another series. And as if lessons hadn't already been learned even Don Lusher suffered a similar fate when his Thames-produced tribute to Ted, "Listen to My Music" was screened at a similarly-ridiculous hour of 10.30 pm.

Now we all know that during the summer months all the television companies operate on a silly-season basis, but as far as ITV was concerned this wasn't silly, it was both ridiculous and irresponsible. It certainly left the impression that both Thames and ATV were not capable of handling such programmes once they had achieved hit status.

Of course there are other television companies which could prove that sentiment wrong some time in the future; that is up to them. Personally, I have doubts about such occasions, and I also have grave reservations about their credibility on such matters.

With "The Jack Parnell Big Band Show" they had the perfect vehicle, and what happened? They blew it! Yes, they let it slip through their fingers and the ever-younger television honchoes were left with egg on their very embarrassed faces. They also seriously jeopardised their knowledge of the importance of such shows.

So, what are the thoughts of Harry Bence today, almost 20 years after the revival seemed to be fast gathering momentum and yet somehow got lost along the way?

"I believe that the love affair between the music of the Forties and the public owes some of its attraction to psychology," he says. "Whenever things get tough, or whenever there's a depression, people fall back on the kind of entertainment that reminds them of a time when there was hope and excitement in their lives."

Harry compares it with a step back into the womb, bringing with it a feeling of security — no matter how temporary. "Personally," he added, "I don't believe with sticking to the original material. I think that it makes it too dated. It's like a new house — it's even better with a fresh coat of paint."

When Ted died in 1969 only a handful of bands remained eeking out a meagre living, with many of them playing at venues which, in their heyday, their leaders would certainly have had second thoughts about.

Syd Lawrence, who has done almost as much to extol the virtues of Glenn Miller's music as Glenn did himself, decided that the time was right to attempt to redress the balance of the music scene away from the pop-dominated vogue.

Syd Lawrence, one of the first big-band revivalists.

The Syd Lawrence Orchestra pictured in concert with two of Ted's former players — Ken Kiddier on the extreme left of the saxophone section, and Ronnie Verrell on drums.

It is of course history how, for amusement, the former licensee of the Railway Hotel in Handforth, Cheshire, and a former trumpeter with the Northern Dance Orchestra, decided to form his own band and play at the Railway on a regular Tuesday-night basis.

As Syd's fame rapidly began to spread, and the audiences increased, his band and its sound soon began to attract those already in the business.

Showman drummer, Eric Delaney, formerly one of Ted's colleagues in his Geraldo days, dropped in one night and had a rare opportunity to flex his muscles (unpaid) on the drums.

Other visitors included Josef Locke and also the late Donald Peers.

"The staggering thing was that not only had I and my colleagues been missing this kind of music, but the general public had been missing it, too," said Syd. "I came along at the right time without realising it."

However, before going on the road on tour, and becoming a national institution along the way, Syd found himself at a crossroads. He could have stayed comfortable with the NDO and continued running the Railway Hotel with his wife, Catherine.

It's reputed that Syd was asked, over a pint, about the possibilities of taking to the road and touring. He just laughed and said: "Not likely! I'd be mad to lose my BBC superannuation — even for Glenn Miller." But take the risk he did: he gave up the pub, resigned from the NDO and the rest is history.

It wasn't long before Syd's sounds aroused the interest of Granada Television, who decided to do an outside broadcast film of the band. The film came over so well that the company decided to make it into a one-hour spectacular to be shown on the ITV network; deja vu? Not quite. That single programme was transmitted in June, 1969, and from then on the band has never looked back.

78

In 1970 the orchestra was established on a national footing as Syd and his musicians, month in and month out, travelled the length and breadth of Great Britain attracting huge audiences and generating tremendous interest in their music.

Touring Europe in top television shows with other stars like Tony Bennett and Johnny Mathis, throughout the Seventies, saw this fine outfit go from one success to another. Forward into the Eighties saw the band undertaking several trips abroad including Canada, Germany, France, Sweden, Switzerland and Holland.

But what is interesting about the Eighties is that during this period Syd took on board two of Ted's top and most popular musicians — baritone saxophonist Ken Kiddier, and Britain's top drummer Ronnie Verrell.

Two very wise and shrewd acquisitions indeed, and which led to the band possessing an albeit small Heath influence. Remember what I said earlier about Ted's dominant and omnipotent force?

■■■■■■■■■■■■■■■■■

Since the days when Syd's band really took off as perhaps the greatest exponents of Glenn Miller's music anywhere in the world, its roll call and its workload are both as impressive and exhausting as you are likely to find anywhere. In fact, its crammed diary of bookings reads almost like a gazetteer.

But after those early beginnings the band appeared to be in danger of being labelled a copy-cat outfit because of its policy of playing note-for-note copies of Miller recordings. Many thought that the band could not survive as long as its policy seemed dedicated to draining the last drop of blood from the Miller archives.

Syd, however, had other ideas, and he proved just what kind of a musical tactician he was when he broadened the band's horizons by including in its repertoire arrangements of, among others, Charlie Barnet, Artie Shaw, Tommy Dorsey, Ray Anthony and, of course, Ted Heath, who he unashamedly refers to as the greatest.

Today that policy speaks for itself inasmuch that his orchestra is far and away the most popular band around and is, perhaps, just as much in demand as was Ted's great outfit of the Fifties and Sixties.

And so to the Nineties . . . Today, Syd's band has been virtually taken over by his prodigy and former pianist, Bryan Pendleton. Syd, although semi-retired, still appears at venues of his choice — those which don't take him too far away from home. He says that he wants to take things easy, yet at the same time keep his fingers on the pulse of the band.

No doubt he will, for his success has proved beyond any arguments that there is still plenty of room in today's world for his kind of music. And with his track record of box-office bookings, plus the fact that Bryan Pendleton is the ideal man to fill his shoes, there's really no need for Syd to worry.

Apart from his near-monopoly of the big-band revival in the early Seventies, another venture took place at about this time and one which sparked off great hopes of a breath of fresh air and a wind of change blowing through the music scene.

Ironically, the incident took place from within the Lawrence camp itself, when a number of his musicians took the monumental decision to quit Syd's employ and start a band of their own. Thus, in 1974, the Million Airs Orchestra was born as a musical co-operative not only creating that much-needed breath of fresh air, but also taking off as if it were about to cause a storm.

In many ways the band was looked upon in terms of scepticism, and was regarded by many as a kind of Syd Lawrence Mark II outfit. To some extent, in its early days at least, this attitude appeared to be justified with the band playing in a similar style, but minus its former leader.

The main difference, however, was that the Million Airs were prepared to experiment in their choice of music and leave Syd with an almost clear field in which to concentrate on reproducing the Glenn Miller style of playing.

But somehow the band always had an enigmatic air about it, as though it were standing at a crossroads and wondering which direction it should take. It was a wonderfully professional outfit, there was no doubt about that. But it also left a lot of people in a state of quandry.

The musicians had big and wonderful ideas and when the Million Airs Concert Orchestra was formed it completed an exhaustive tour of the British Isles, taking in 40 venues, and recreating the legendary sounds of Glenn Miller's AEF Orchestra. Many will doubtless recall the success of the orchestra's concert at the Royal Albert Hall in December, 1975.

The tour was the outcome of that triumphant night and it gave the rest of the country the opportunity to get a sample of what the AEF was all about — and the Million Airs. The concerts were extremely well-balanced and represented faithfully the music so very much associated with Miller and the AEF.

But I have to admit that when I left one of these concerts, at the Davenport Theatre, Stockport, I did so with nothing short of a concerned and thoughtful hangover. To me, at that particular moment, the direction of the Million Airs was arguable: did they have any intentions of developing a forte of their own, or were they going to become yet another troupe trudging down the Glenn Miller road? If the latter was to be the case, then what a waste!

With the talent and versatility contained within the ranks of the band it seemed such a pity that it was all, apparently, being channeled in the direction of a figure who became a musical legend in his own right.

However, when you took the Million Airs away from the music of Miller, and left them to their own devices, the end product was a refreshing and appealing sound which smacked of an individuality that was sadly missing from the big-band scene. Theirs was a sound which should have been nurtured rather than shelved in favour of a sound that was already instantly recognisable.

With many acclaiming the Million Airs as one of the top bands in Europe this should have been used as a foundation for them to build up a reputation for that individual improvisation, and at the same time help to dispel the theory that they were nothing more than a band of carbon-copy also-rans.

For the band to have slid into that descriptive bracket would have been a pity, but not an impossibility. Naturally enough it was often compared with the Syd Lawrence outfit, but there can be no two Syd Lawrences just as there could be no two Glenn Millers.

So, were the Million Airs on a musical hiding-to-nothing, with an invisible albatross hanging around their necks?

With all the good will in the world it seemed that a dedicated concentration on Miller's music would prove to be an achilles heel to any orchestra. To the outside observer that certainly proved to be the case. But from the insiders (those who obviously knew better) it was suggested from various quarters of the big-band business that the sooner the organisation took steps to sign the pledge, the better.

To coin a well-hackneyed cliche: "The world is everyone's oyster", and as far as the Million Airs were concerned they were no exception to this rule. After all, the big-band front had been, and always will be, minus a dominant force since the chasm left by Ted Heath. And, even after all this time, since Ted's death, that chasm is still there.

The big-band world has cried out for an outfit to attempt to emulate the heights which Ted's band reached — without the necessity to copy. For the Million Airs to have devoted their energies in that direction would not, as many have since argued, have been a waste of time. Musically and professionally they were perfectly equipped to take up just such a challenge — as some of the tracks on the band's first two albums proved.

Tracks from their "Introducing the Million Airs" album showed that the band's treatment of numbers like "The Champ" (a real Ted Heath warhorse) "Concerto For Clarinet", "Holiday For Trombones" and a gloriously-breezy and effervescent version of John Lennon and Paul McCartney's "Norwegian Wood" enabled a very obvious and distinctive Heath-style sound to come across successfully.

Experimentation to the band at this stage was vital if it was to maintain the exciting promise which it first displayed on formation. On the sleeve of this album Alan Dell wrote:

"It's a rare thing, but the Million Airs are a co-operative unit. They have all shared the struggling months of their launching, and now I think they can look forward to an increasingly-successful future, with a following that must surely grow with every passing week. Because this is a really excellent big band with a wide musical scope."

That was all very well and to that end they, and everyone else, should have known exactly where they were going. But no one did. Not even the band. It seemed that everyone was in a state of limbo. All hoped of course that the sooner that state was revolved the better it would be all round, for all thoughts were for the future of the band.

Former Heath altoist Harry Bence, who also made a big-band revival attempt fronting the New Squadronaires.

Would it take an A-road to international stardom (which it deserved) or would it plump for a B-road which, after a few dance dates and the not-too-prestigious concert, would eventually lead it into relative obscurity?

Sadly, at the crossroads, the Million Airs chose the latter — who knows whether it was by accident or design? Maybe it was a question of finance, internal politics or whatever. The only positive thing to emerge from it all was that the B-road led to the eventual disbanding of an orchestra which had possessed such high potential, a rapidly-growing band of followers and a seemingly lucrative future.

In short, and without attempting to enter into any kind of unsubstantiated speculation of the situation, the fairy-tale story of the band was killed off by the giant, and a really worthwhile big-band revival attempt bit the dust.

Despite the promising revival attempt of the Seventies, and its initial spiralling tones of success in relation to Syd Lawrence, the minor success of the Million Airs and the latter anomolies relating to Jack Parnell's valiant efforts and his raw television deal (and let there be no doubts that Jack was short-changed) these men, and the musicians, played a very crucial role in the upsurge of a renewed and vigorous interest in the big bands.

Maybe it was a contrast of fortunes — exposure-wise, that is. But there's one thing which is indisputable: they WERE in the right place at the right time. And because problems of various kinds cropped up from many quarters, it certainly did not kill off the interest nor, I hasten to add, will it ever. Just bear in mind those words of Harry Bence earlier on in the chapter.

82

However, the disappointments of the various revival attempts did not altogether make for a picture of doom and gloom. The Million Airs had, after all, made a spirited, valiant and not unsuccessful try; Harry Bence had jogged the memories of the nation with his band, the New Squadronaires, and here again it was not without a fair share of success. And it was certainly no fault of Jack's that his programme was given the elbow.

But, there is an old saying that you can't keep a good Heath man down! How true that sentiment certainly is. For out of the band ashes of the Seventies rose not one Phoenix, but two — and both involved the genial and gentlemanly Don Lusher, the man who personifies all the styles of leadership, discipline, dedication and integrity which the maestro stood for.

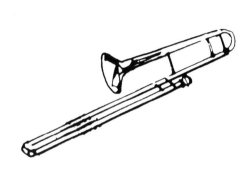

CHAPTER SEVEN

The Natural Successor

As I have said elsewhere in this book I feel extremely privileged to have known Don for as many years as I have, and it always gives me as much pleasure now when I see him in action on stage as it did that very first time back in 1953. Having worked for various newspapers, and reported on many, many concerts in the North-West when Don has been fronting the Heath band, I still never fail to experience the same strange feeling.

Perhaps strange is a rather strong word to use, but seeing him leading this great band of musicians is like watching Ted in action all over again. It all somehow makes for a rather pleasantly, scary sensation, for not only is Don's inspired discipline so obvious (as was Ted's), but his whole style of presentation is so uncannily similar to that of his former employer.

The man is so professional and articulate in everything he does that it's small wonder he was held in such high regard by Ted, and is so very much in demand by others in the music business — musicians of the status of Henry Mancini, Billy May, Michel Legrand, Artie Shaw and Robert Farnon, to name but a few. So it must also not have come as much of a surprise, either, when Mrs Moira Heath asked Don to take charge and become the musical director of the reformed Ted Heath band back in 1976.

When he was asked by Moira to perform this function it meant that he would have to wear two hats; for at that particular time Don, too, was very instrumental in the big-band revival scene — which was then at an exciting stage — with his own Don Lusher Big Band.

But to be honoured with the request of taking hold of the reins of the musical legacy which Ted had left behind, following his death, meant that it was a mission which he could not possibly refuse, and a challenge that most musicians would have given their eye teeth for. Moira, and the rest of Ted's family, wanted both the name and the music of Ted Heath to live on, and in their eyes Don Lusher was the only man suitable to do that particular and formidable job.

Seeing Don lead the Ted Heath band seems to add to the feeling that the maestro is still around

Don Lusher, the man with the 'smoothest trombone in the business', one of the most respected musicians in the world and the leader and musical director of the Ted Heath Band today.

One of the most interesting aspects of Don's choices of personnel, not for his own band but for the Heath assembly, was the selection of an excellent young trombonist by the name of Chris Dean.

I say interesting because with his inclusion in Don's band there is nothing out of place.

However, when you see Chris sitting in the trombone section of the Ted Heath band he does, at first glance, appear to look a little out of place surrounded as he is by the elder statesmen of the Heath era.

But it all becomes crystal clear when Don performs the band introductions to the audiences.

When the time comes for Chris to take a bow Don always enlightens them, and clears up the mystery of why Chris just happens to be sitting there.

Chris Dean

Don says: "Chris Dean is a young man who wasn't even born when this band was younger and in its prime. But, had he been around then, Ted would almost certainly have snapped him up with both hands. He was destined to play in this band."

A first-class testimony indeed to Buxton-born Chris (how the name of that town keeps cropping up!) who played for a number of years with Syd Lawrence and then the Les Howard-directed Northern Dance Orchestra, before becoming a session musician and then teaming up with Don.

Chris wasn't even born when Ted's all-star band was in its prime

Don fronting his own Don Lusher Big Band, with a number of the musicians who played in Ted's outfit.

I once remember writing an article about Ted for an international music magazine in 1976, and also being invited to talk about him on a big-band programme on BBC Radio Manchester. I was asked by the presenter, John Richards, to sum up what my feelings were regarding the success of Ted, so I used the same prognosis as that for the article.

I concluded both by saying: "There has never been a band so unique, so polished, so professional and so popular as that of Ted Heath's. The sad truth of the matter is that there never will be again, either."

Well since then events have proved how wrong you can be, for at that time I had reckoned without Don, who was to prove more than just one of the main attractions in Ted's all-embracing and all-star band.

Moira, in her determination to keep Ted's memory alive, asked Don to take over the band as musical director.

As already said, he could hardly refuse really, seeing as how Moira had made the request on the stage during a concert at the Fairfield Hall, Croydon, in front of a packed audience.

In his book Don writes: "Whilst giving a Ted Heath concert at the Fairfield Hall, Croydon, in 1976, we were nearly at the end where I was thanking everyone concerned, when I was aware of some activity at the side of the stage.

"As I looked round I saw Moira Heath walking towards me carrying a trombone.

Tailor-made to keep

a legend alive

IT had to take a man of exceptional qualities to take over the mantle of the Ted Heath band, after the leader's death in 1969.

With Don Lusher there was not a finer choice, for in many ways his gentlemanly manner, coupled with his no-nonsense style of leadership, bears a more than remarkable resemblance to those of his former employer.

Although Don's ideas are different, he says that he bears in mind all the time what Ted would have wanted — his likes and dislikes. And yet in no way does he try to copy him.

But Don, like Ted, is a stickler for starting a concert dead on time, and admits that even after all these years the famous signature tune, "Listen To My Music", still never ceases to thrill him.

Just like his ex-boss he is a perfectionist leader and respected by everyone in the big-band business — further proof that Don Lusher is the ideal man for the job, and tailor-made to keep the sounds of a true musical legend well and truly alive.

"I couldn't imagine what was going on, but I was soon to find out. In front of a packed house, and with all those wonderful musicians behind me, she presented me with Ted's old trombone, inscribed on the bell: *"Presented to Don Lusher on November 9, 1976, Ted Heath's trombone with thanks for perpetuating his memory."*

"Moira made a moving speech; I was speechless and caught completely off guard. It is a great honour to have the trombone, and I shall treasure it for the rest of my life."

I know how you feel, Don. I have the same feelings with regards to a pair of drum sticks given to me by Ronnie Verrell.

When Ted died so, too, did a legend — in every sense of the word. But he left behind a legacy; an institution backed up by the personnel who progressed through the ranks under his leadership. Think of a musician — a name musician — of today and the chances are that a link with Ted Heath is there, for many of those same musicians are still playing with the Heath band only this time under Don's direction — a man right out of the Heath mould itself.

This is further proof, if it is needed, as to why Moira entrusted the man to uphold her late husband's legacy.

Four years ago, at Manchester's Free Trade Hall, the band played the sounds of Ted's music over the past 40 years, with nearly all the personnel of that era who played with the universally-known leader. It was akin to experiencing the effects of being in a time-warp.

For various reasons over the years, including illness, I had been unable to see the band whenever it came to my neck of the woods, and so I lost touch with the visits. But I was able to pick up the threads when I joined the Oldham Evening Chronicle and was able to review the concerts again for the paper.

There on stage that night were the stalwarts of Heath bands gone by: Jack, Kenny, Tommy, Ronnie Chamberlain, Henry, the late Norman Stenfalt and Bill Geldard, together with Ted's former singers Lita and Dennis.

Pedigree artists all, with that essential staying power, which is why they are still around today playing to packed venues and adding credence to any arguments about whether or not there is a renaissaance taking place in the world of big-band music. This staying-power factor is even more remarkable when you consider the overall age of the band's musicians.

When Jack left his kit to come down to the microphone to sing (sorry, Jack, is that what you call it!) one of his best-known numbers, "Route 66", he first had a friendly little chat with the audience. This is something which he always does, as well as tell one of his favourite jokes. A great comedian is Jack.

After the joke, which I seem to recall was about him being booed by a Peeping Tom, Jack told the audience that before going out on stage that night he'd been doing a spot of mental arithmetic, and he'd worked out that "the total age of this bunch is two thousand, two hundred and something . . ."

90

What the Papers Said . . .

A Lusher memory of Ted

MORE than 40 years ago, band leader Ted Heath adopted a simple philosophy to achieve his ambition of fronting Britain's best and foremost swing band.

The philosophy was to surround himself with the best musicians in the land. In doing so, he achieved something more — his band soon became recognised as not only the best in this country, but also the world.

In short, the best played for the best.

Last night's concert was not only about nostalgia, it was about longevity. Under the direction of Don Lusher, who took over the band at the request of Ted's widow, Moira, the Heath name has now become an institution, with nearly all of the musicians from those early days still playing.

THE TED HEATH BAND
(Davenport Theatre, Stockport)

Their names are almost as familiar as the numbers they played, and just as instantly recognisable — Kenny Baker, Tommy Whittle, Jack Parnell, Duncan Campbell and Ronnie Chamberlain, to name only five.

They, along with singer Lita Roza, made a mockery of their ages as they relived the numbers of the band's musical library, with skills and disciplines which were such an essential and vital part of Ted Heath's academy of professionalism.

Long-term favourites included "Hot Toddy", "The Faithful Hussar", "Body and Soul" and "Hawaiian War Chant".

They delivered a wave of nostalgia, but, more importantly, underlined the era of a band which swept all before it, with hit records, world tours and regular Sunday-night swing sessions at the London Palladium.

It would be an extremely hard task to attempt to single out anyone. But the rule hardly applies here, for this band has always had one of equality.

There is no doubt whatsoever that Mrs Heath made an excellent choice in her selection of the ultra-professional Don Lusher as the name to uphold her husband's musical legacy.

His style of leadership really is on a parallel with that of Ted and I am happy to report that the best are still playing for the best.

T.P.

Big, bold and British

THIS was the British band which, in true swinging fashion, 40 years ago, proved the cornerstone and inspiration for all the other big bands in this country.

It swept all before it, conquered America, then went on to challenge and, in the opinion of many, became better, than most in the world. That in no way is a mark of disrespect for the band's great US counterparts of the era such as Stan Kenton, Count Basie and Duke Ellington.

True, they were dynamic and elite bands with absolutely nothing to prove, and their names were held in awe. But the all-star Ted Heath aggregation became an institution — a musical family — which has lasted long after Ted's death in 1969.

Under the direction of master trombonist Don Lusher, who has been associated with the band over all those years, it has to be said that this is most definitely not another of

THE TED HEATH BAND
(Free Trade Hall, Manchester

those ghost outfits which carries on trading on the name of the leader.

With a few exceptions, the members of the band are now senior, and jokingly describe themselves as the "bus-pass brigade". But their talents are by no means a joke, being a joy to both watch and listen to.

Ambassador

For example, can there possibly be a more distinctive-sounding tenor saxist than Tommy Whittle around today, or a more melodic trumpeter than Kenny Baker?

Certainly, there is no finer trombone ambassador in the business than Lusher, and no better example than drummer Jack Parnell of a

laid-back and thinking man's approach to his craft.

As far as vocalists go they don't come any more durable than Dennis Lotis and Lita Roza — who boasted having been 42 years with the band and who was quite philosophical in her own rather whimsical way about getting old.

Without any doubt, as far as the audience was concerned, this was a concert for the purists, who were treated to a vast and contrasting range of numbers from the famed Heath repertoire.

The final, swinging show-stopper, "Heading North", prompted the observation that the band should head north more often.

When assessing the outfit of today there is still no other even remotely close and, although attempting to avoid the use of a cliche, the band is still like a vintage wine and getting better with age.
T.P.

Reproduced by permission of the Oldham Evening Chronicle.

Translated that meant an average age of about 60. Even Lita boasted that night of possessing a bus-pass and, quite openly, amusingly and with tongue-in-cheek declared that at 60 she was now "a born-again virgin". Dennis on the other hand reckoned that he had one or two more years to wait for his pass!

But even now, ages aside and after all these years, the Heath band is still the tops — the yardstick for the rest of the established bands, and also the up-and-coming ones, including that very talented young man-of-the-moment, trombonist Andy Prior, who unreservedly is on record as proclaiming Ted's band as the best ever.

So just why was Don chosen as the man to musically direct and keep alive the memory of Ted's band, not only for the family but for the many thousands of admirers of the Heath legend? And what were his credentials for taking on such a seemingly impossible task?

Well the job was not as awe-inspiring to Don as at first might be imagined, or as difficult as it could have been for someone else to take up the responsibility of such a mighty challenge. For the simple reason was that the two men shared a number of things in common.

The two most striking examples which spring instantly to mind are that they were both trombonists, and both played with Geraldo's orchestra. But perhaps the most important aspect of Moira's choice was that Don possesses the same kind of leadership qualities as Ted had, and also has the same kind of attitude and demands; punctuality, discipline (both on and off stage) and above all the vital and essential ingredients of musicianship and professionalism.

Just like Jack did in his ill-fated television series, Don surrounds himself in his own band with more than a goodly share of his ex-Heath colleagues including Tommy Whittle, Derek Watkins, Kenny Baker and Tony Fisher, and who do more than blend in well with the other fine musicians like Ray Swinfield, Colin Sheen, Chris Dean and pianist Ronnie Price.

Incidentally, Ronnie was Don's best man when he married Diana, a lovely, friendly and highly-efficient lady who helps to take most of the weight off Don's shoulders when it comes to making a number of the necessary arrangements when the two bands go on tour.

My good friend Derek Boulton, who kindly wrote the introduction to this book and is the managing director of Horatio Nelson Records — Don's recording label — has his own theories about Don and the band, and which are not a million miles away from my own.

"I believe a lot in spiritualism," he says, "and I think Ted looks down on us and guides us. Moira, too, feels very strongly on this. Don, to me, is a replica of Ted: he's fussy, he's firm and he's very professional, and these are the sort of things that attract me to him — apart from him being a most wonderful and great player. There's not a trombone player in this country to touch him, and I'll even go as far as saying that there isn't a player in America who can touch him, either. They might think they can, but not consistently.

"When I get people like Robert Farnon telling me to make sure that Don is available for one of his recording sessions, then that speaks volumes. Before an album recording session of Bob's, with George Shearing, he had written a trombone piece and he rang me to make sure that Don was there to play it, or it wouldn't be included.

"Don is a little different from Ted in his attitude to the programming because he also picks up his money from his work with the brass bands, his musical colleges, his jazz sessions with the Best of British, guest spots and, of course, his own band. He doesn't want to be a replica of the Heath band: he wants to do his own scene, otherwise it would mean a replica of the nostalgia of the Heath band all the time — and that's not what we want.

THE TED HEATH ORCHESTRA

DIRECTED BY

DON LUSHER

WILL APPEAR IN CONCERT AT THE HUDDERSFIELDTOWN HALL

SATURDAY 23 SEPTEMBER

AT 7.30 PM
WITH GUEST ARTISTS
LITA ROSA & DENNIS LOTIS

ALSO FEATURING
KENNY BAKER JACK PARNELL
TOMMY WHITTLE RONNIE CHAMBERLAIN
HENRY MACKENZIE & DUNCAN CAMPBELL

A familiar sight every year on the billboards of about a dozen selected venues up and down the country.

"But I think basically that Don is the nearest thing that you'll ever get to Ted: he's well organised, his wife Diana stage manages and these people are a dream to be associated with. Because if you say 'do something', they're going to do it.

"Ted always used to say to me: 'You've got to be a brass player to run a band successfully.' I think that particular sentence sums up the credentials of Don Lusher."

To add further strength to those credentials, Don possesses in his home the entire Heath library of music scores and he was forced to have special cupboards built in his office to accommodate the bulk of those manuscripts — because there is so much of it! Also, he stores Ted's original music stands which the band uses on its shows.

Good organisation is paramount to Don, which means that when the Heath band gets a booking his first job is to round up 18 musicians and singers for the occasion. If all are available Don's next job is to go through the musical library to select a programme which will illustrate the various periods of the band's history — rather than just sticking to the same material all the time.

Don says that some times this is easier said than done, for some of the manuscripts are so old that they can hardly be read; in some cases parts or even pages are missing and, worse, some of the scores are lost. Probably, because Don is a non-smoker, browsing through this library can be quite an ordeal for him, for all the music reeks of cigarette smoke and this can cause quite a whiff when he opens the store cupboard, as you can well imagine.

On the day of the concert Don is as meticulous as Ted was: he visits the venue to set out the stands with the band manager and he helps to iron out any snags which may be prevalent. He then takes the band through a 3-hour rehearsal, pushing the band all the time on account of the time factor. Like Ted, Don gives his men a suitable rest period in order for them to relax and change comfortably before the concert.

Although Ted's system was, in some instances different than Don's, the two men's ideas follow along a somewhat similar track of thought. In Ted's case he always kept an envelope in his car, and if he thought of anything connected with the concert he would write it down at the earliest moment.

Don, on the other hand, goes over his already-prepared announcements in the silence of his dressing room — having already rehearsed them while driving to the concert. When all this has been gone over time and again, and it's almost time to face the audience, Don is no different at all to Ted when it comes to quietly wondering if everything will work out smoothly.

The time is right and the cue to start comes from the stage manager — dead on time . . . as always. The band strikes up with "Listen To My

The glamorous Sheila Southern, one of this country's most talented singers, adds a special and highly-attractive bonus in her role as vocalist with Don's band.

Music", the signature tune which Ted wrote and which thrills all who have ever been associated with the Heath band.

Don himself admits: "This opener never ceases to thrill me. What a thrill it is to stand in front of this great band of musicians and listen to that sound. I don't try to copy Ted in any way, but I do bear in mind all the time what he would have wanted — his likes and dislikes."

This is no small wonder, really, for the genial Don Lusher is, as long as he leads that band, walking in the footsteps of the maestro. In other words, he really *is* a natural successor.

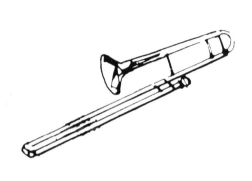

CHAPTER EIGHT

Memories of the Maestro

When it comes to memories of Ted every reader will have his or her own particular one to look back upon, and the same when it comes to paying personal tributes. In my own particular case, and being the vehement big-band enthusiast that I am, I must say that I was both surprised and delighted to receive an invitation from Radio Cavell, the Royal Oldham Hospital radio station, to appear on one of its Sunday afternoon programmes called "Sounds of the Big Band Era." last November.

To my mind voluntary work has a happy habit of bringing its own rewards, especially when it is unexpected and deeply and personally satisfying. This was made abundantly clear to me when I unhesitatingly accepted an invitation from the presenter of the show, Harvey Crossland, who has been associated with the programme for more than 5 years.

To be invited on to this programme was like feeding the proverbial donkey with strawberries, and Harvey and I met up beforehand to discuss what form our joint presentation should take. To my modest credit I suggested that we should entertain the patients with a musical tribute to Ted, to mark the anniversary of his death.

Radio Cavell, one of the country's oldest hospital radio stations, is most certainly not the BBC or independent radio, nor does it have any great pretensions. However, the dedication and application of those who put out the programmes cannot be questioned and would certainly be the equal of most who are employed in some of those organisations.

There is also a feeling of affinity in work of this nature for those, like myself, who have ever been forced to spend time in hospital, those headphones at the back of the bed can at times prove to be invaluable, especially when there is both a friendly and personal touch applied to the programmes.

Harvey Crossland is a presenter who knows exactly what the big-band business is all about, because for 10 years he was a drummer with a resident band at a local ballroom in Oldham.

It was he who was the mastermind and the driving force behind a link-up last year between Oldham's Queen Elizabeth Hall and the hospital. The occasion was a visit to the town by the Herb Miller Orchestra, as part of a 48-venue British tour, and through Harvey's efforts the hospital patients were treated to live big-band music, Glenn Miller style.

The preparation and the detail of our tribute programme to Ted was almost as important as the presentation itself, and we tried to leave no stone unturned in the search for something approaching perfection. For example, a couple of weeks previously Harvey and I compiled a programme script and contacted Mrs Moira Heath, along with Don Lusher.

Making music . . . John Miller (left) nephew of Glenn Miller and leader of the Herb Miller Orchestra, Jonathan Bailey, the orchestra manager and Harvey Crossland. They are pictured in the studios of Radio Cavell.

Both willingly responded to our idea, with Don sending a personally-recorded greeting and Moira a written message which was read out to the patients. Almost immediately afterwards, as a gesture of appreciation from us, we sent them both a cassette recording of the programme. The musical tribute, enveloped in our script, included about 18 classic numbers from the vast library of Ted's music and included "Opus One", "Hot Toddy", "The Champ", "Swinging Shepherd Blues" and "Lush Slide", together with between-record narrative.

In Studio 2, before the live 5 pm broadcast, we did a quick run-through of the script, checked the sound levels and arranged the playing sequence of the records. It was then a case of on with the headphones and bang on the hour, after an introduction from studio manager Nigel Hobson, we were on the air to the strains of Ted's signature tune, "Listen To My Music"

But it was one of the quickest-passing hours on record (if you'll pardon the pun) and we were all too soon fading out the programme with the same number that we opened with. It was hoped that our musical efforts were appreciated, for there are some who would say that it didn't really matter as it was only hospital radio after all.

But patients are people, and to my mind they are a very special and important breed of listener. They more than most deserve to be properly entertained, and at Radio Cavell they are treated to such considerations with both enthusiasm and skill in plentiful supply.

As for me, well I'm getting a bit too long in the tooth to be trendy, but it was this participation for the benefit of the more mature patients (and hopefully for some of the younger ones, too), coupled with the opportunity to spin some of my favourite Ted Heath tracks, which proved to be the most satisfying element.

99

One of the most popular of Ted's musicians just happened to be the smallest, and because he was so small he very nearly didn't make it into the band at all. And not to put too fine a point on it I've always wondered how a drummer the size of **Ronnie Verrell** can possess so much explosive and magnetic power behind the skins.

However, don't be fooled; Ronnie can, and always has been able to, produce the goods. But it took Ted more than one occasion to be convinced of this, before he finally took Ronnie into his employ in 1952.

In a quiet moment in the bandroom at Stockport's Davenport Theatre, where we have met many, many times before when he has visited the venue with the Syd Lawrence Orchestra, Rochester-born Ronnie told me how he was both overlooked and dismissed the first time that Ted saw and heard him.

"I joined the band in 1952, but about 2½ or 3 years earlier I had an audition with Ted. Jack Parnell was the drummer then, and it was during a rehearsal at the Hammersmith Palais. I got an audition because Jack, who wanted to leave the band, had seen me playing at Gillingham with a local band and had recommended me to Ted.

"Now Jack's a very tall man and I had to use his drums. I could hardly reach the pedals because the whole kit was adjusted for a giant, and I'm not a giant man! Apart from that handicap, I was also very nervous because Ted stood over me almost all of the time. I read the part alright, but I must have looked terribly frightened."

Afterwards, Ted's verdict on the audition was: "He plays very well, but he's too small — he has no personality."

Ronnie Verrell didn't land the job and so Jack was persuaded to stay. But it wasn't all bad news because Ronnie was offered a job with Cyril Stapleton and went on the road with his band, undertook broadcasts and recordings and gained the confidence and experience which comes from playing before large crowds.

"When news came along the grapevine that Jack again wanted to leave, I received a panic call," recalled Ronnie. "Jack was ill, Ted couldn't get anyone else and so he asked me if I'd do a Sunday Night Swing Session at the Palladium. By this time I'd got the confidence, so I did it. For me it went down very well indeed, and later Ted offered me the job."

As a number of the members of the Lawrence orchestra engaged themselves in a card school before the show, he lit up a Marlboro and inhaled deeply. Now was the time to bring something of a slander out into the open.

Ted was always on the look-out for the very best musicians and singers for his band, and his search for talent never ended.

He sought the formula that would make his outfit not only a good one, but the best that this country had ever produced.

Having got the personnel of his choice his ambition was successful, thanks to dedication, hard work and the desire to succeed.

Ted knew that he was the master of the business and so, too, did everyone else.

Ronnie Verrell, arguably the best drummer that this country has ever produced, and who joined Ted's band in 1952. He stayed for 15 years ... but he almost didn't get the job because he was on the small side.

Star trumpeter Kenny Baker, who was with Ted's band from the beginning in 1945, and whose connections with the Heath organisation span almost 50 years.

101

I asked Ronnie if he'd set the record straight regarding a long-standing rumour that Ted had actually (quote) 'stolen' him from Cyril Stapleton. He was adamant about putting that particular slice of mischief to rest.

"He didn't steal me! Look, here was the top band in the country: if you wanted to better yourself you went for it. Cyril came up to me, when I gave him notice, and said: 'Why does everyone want to join Ted Heath?' So I said that Ted was actually doubling my money. Cyril followed up with: 'Why didn't you tell me!' It was the old bandleader's line! 'Why didn't you tell me!'"

But Cyril made it very hard for Ronnie at the time by insisting that he honour the agreement and serve three-months notice — hoping that Ted wouldn't wait. But he did wait for his man, and after Jack left to form his own band Ted brought in Basil Kirchin for the period before Ronnie joined.

"Basil proved to be a popular stand-in with the band and it took me quite a while to get friendly with the guys," said Ronnie. "They thought it was a dirty trick, but eventually I was accepted and I spent 15 of the happiest years of my life with Ted and the lads."

Basil Kirchin later joined up with his father, Ivor, to form the Kirchin Band — a combo which specialised in exciting mambo and Latin-American rhythms, and which proved to be highly popular in the Fifties.

███████████████

Along with everyone else connected with the Heath band, and the successful tours of the States, Ronnie has his own very fond memories. "We were all nervous about that first tour, but we caused a storm over there. At Carnegie Hall we received a standing ovation for about six minutes; we all felt so proud for Ted and we were all in tears. We had done it — we'd conquered it. It was such a massively-good band.

"I remember the first number of that concert was 'Kings Cross Climax' and we were all very nervous. I was sweating like mad before we started and I asked Bobby Pratt to give me a drop of Scotch to help calm me down. I was still sweating with fear and had to hold the sticks as tightly as possible in case they flew out of my hand, via the sweat. Fortunately it worked out OK.

"By the time we came to the second number, 'Memories of You', which was a duet between Bobby and Bert Ezzard, it took the roof off — it really broke the ice. The audience liked the first number, but when they heard Bert and Bobby blowing higher and higher we just relaxed after that. We knew the crowd was with us.

"But what a package we had! Nat King Cole, the Four Freshmen, June Christy — Stan Kenton's singer — and a comedian, Gary Morton. I tell you, it felt very flat when we came back to England, what with all the adrenalin flowing from the applause we received over there.

Ted's first drummer, Jack Parnell, whose television series "The Jack Parnell Big Band Show" was such a hit in the Seventies. Today he is still a vitally important part of the Heath band, which is now led and directed by Don Lusher.

"We went back to the States on two other occasions — once when we were backing Al Hibbler. Remember him? He had a big hit with 'Unchained Melody'. The other time we were backing Carmen Macrae. I was very, very lucky that I happened to be in the right place at the right time, and part of such a marvellous outfit. It was the happiest time ever."

By virtue of an anecdote which I had read in Don Lusher's autobiography* there was something that I had to ask Ronnie, regarding the night when he failed to pack a pair of black socks for a concert. Worse still was the fact that none of the other members of the band had a spare pair to lend him. His eyes twinkled as he lit another cigarette.

"That's a true story — it's perfectly true! My left foot as you know plays the hi-hat and the bottom of my leg was exposed so that you could see my sock. But that night I didn't have a sock! And because I'd heard that Ted once sacked a guy — I think it was Johnnie Gray — for having a shirt button missing I started to panic.

"So, you know what I did? A true story. I painted my white leg with Cherry Blossom black boot polish. How about that? It was a terrible mess all around the bottoms and inside my trousers, but I had to go on with something black — anything! But I got away with it. Ted didn't know anything about it and I never told him!"

By now it was time for Ronnie to leave and change for the evening's performance, and perhaps after our chat he was quietly keeping his fingers crossed hoping that he'd packed his black socks in his travelling bag. Fortunately they were there!

In bringing the first half of the concert to a close the Syd Lawrence orchestra paid its own tribute to Gene Krupa, with Ronnie giving one of his marvellous solos on "Drummin' Man". After the show Ronnie presented me with the sticks which he had used on that number. Needless to say I shall treasure those battered and well-hammered pieces of maple not only as a memento from one of the world's greatest drummers, but as a souvenir from a dear and long-time friend.

*The Don Lusher Book (Egon Publishers)

In the same year that I first made acquaintance with Ted, I also met the lady who was the top band singer of the day — although I didn't meet her on the first occasion, but on a later date that year.

Lita Roza was the stunner whose eye every hot-blooded male in her audiences tried to catch — including mine! Liverpool-born Lita had style, talent, excellent presentation and a good singing voice, and she stayed with Ted's band for 4½ years after making her debut on February 12, 1950.

That particular day, Lita told me, is one that she'll never forget. "I could sing and didn't think that I was too bad; I was also ambitious. I set my sights high and wanted to sing with the top band, and there was no band around that could top Ted," she said.

Singer Lita Roza who joined Ted's band in 1950 shortly after an awe-inspiring audition at the London Palladium.

Still There Over the Years

Lita as she is today — still glamorous and still singing with the Ted Heath band, with a fine voice that has changed little over the years.

"I'd been living in America for about 5 years and I was over here for a holiday. I decided to write to Ted for an audition, and he sent for me to go along to the Palladium for a rehearsal for one of the Sunday swing sessions. Ted liked what he heard and so I sang with the band that night, but I didn't join it as a regular straight away.

"Ted had started his own London agency in Albermarle Street and he asked me if I'd join, with Ted collecting 10 per cent from whatever bookings or broadcasts he arranged for me. I had to wait for a while before joining the band proper.

"I was living in London at the time and one night I got a call from Ted at about midnight, asking me if I could get down to Torquay the next morning. The band had a two-week booking down there at the Spa, and Ted wanted me to join. I got there, sang, and stayed with the band until 1954.

It was at this time that Lita became Britain's top girl singer and was voted into that position for six consecutive years, before she left to go solo and was offered a recording contract with Decca Records. During this period she appeared and topped the bill at every major theatre in Great Britain.

"When I signed that contract Decca gave me a free hand to choose my own songs, my own arrangers and also my own backing band. I chose the best when I recorded "Allentown Jail", with Reg Owen's arrangement and who else but Ted and the boys backing me."

Lita says that she always regarded Ted as something more than merely an employer — describing him as a father figure who was forever protective, and who drove her in his car to engagements instead of allowing her to travel on the band coach. She says that as a disciplinarian she never heard Ted shout or raise his voice once during the whole of the 4 years that she was with the band. But he knew what he wanted and he also let his musicians know exactly what standards he expected, so that there could never be any excuse if someone stepped out of line.

But, says Lita, in his role as protector he once suffered a terrible disappointment while he was driving her to a booking which the band had in Lincoln one evening.

"In those days Ted drove a beautiful Humber Super Snipe which he thought the world of. As we were driving to Lincoln that day we stopped at a cafe for a cup of tea and a snack in a narrow-streeted town — I think it was Grantham — with Ted parking the car half on the pavement so as not to cause an obstruction.

"I'll never forget the crestfallen look on his face when we came out of the cafe and discovered that a lorry had passed too close and had collided with Ted's car, scraping it all the way along from back to front. It was still driveable, but it was a terrible mess."

When I asked Lita what was the highlight of her time spent with the band, she summed it up in three words: "Meeting Ronnie Hughes." Ronnie, of course, was a member of Ted's trumpet section who, as everyone knows, became the envy of thousands of Lita's male admirers when he married her.

When the war years had ended many new publications were introduced as one of the ways in restoring the nation's morale. Above is one of them, but just make a note of the price. Happy days!

These days Lita still appears with the Ted Heath band, alongside fellow singer Dennis Lotis, on its annual tour of about a dozen selected venues. The difference now is that she has added an amusing, self-mocking accent to her act and, tinged with tones of nostalgia, it is one that still pleases her audiences — especially when she reflects, between songs, on what she describes as "the good old days", and her present-day acquisition of a bus-pass!

Whether this latter possession is one which she mentions out of regret or personal pride is open to speculation, but Lita never fails to mention that the best years of her life were those which she spent with Ted.

As with Lita's comments, about Ted being a father-figure, another person to echo those sentiments is trumpeter **Stan Roderick** who worked with him when they were both members of the Geraldo orchestra in 1943, and who described Ted as a friendly man with a shrewd musical ear.

"It was at this time when Ted told me of his dreams to have a super band after the war. I thought it was maybe just a pipe-dream; but we all know differently now, don't we?" said Stan.

"I was invited to join the original line-up in 1945 and there were no guarantees of regular work in the first few months. We did some 'Music While You Work' broadcasts for the BBC, and other broadcasts as well. In a very short while we were beginning to be recognised as a wonderful new band.

"Ted liked the band to be as immaculate in appearance as the sound of his music. He liked his musicians to be well dressed and of good behaviour. I can recall that there were never any problems with this ruling on our engagements, for we had too much respect for both the man and his music. Any celebrating was strictly *after* the show, and no one ever broke this particular rule."

Stan Roderick, pictured during his days as a member of Ted's trumpet section.

Stan left the band to concentrate on studio work, and also to spend more time with his family. Sadly, he says, he missed out on the prestige tours of the States agreeing that they were a crowning boost for the band. Now in his Seventies, Stan continued with studio work for the next 30 years working for musicians like Robert Farnon, Laurie Johnson and John Barry.

He was also chosen for the line-ups of visiting musical directors for film, music and television recordings working for Henry Mancini, Michel Legrand, Leonard and Elmer Bernstein, Quincy Jones and Don Costa. Also for 12 years Stan was lead trumpet with Frank Sinatra on his yearly visits to Britain and his continental tours.

"But I still have this precious regard for those 6 years which I spent with Ted," says Stan. "We were all in our Twenties and our hearts were full of music, with the determination to succeed whatever the odds. I think my own special highlight was when I was asked by Ted's daughter, Valerie, to play at Ted's funeral at Stoke Poges, at the suggestion of Don Lusher.

"I was asked originally to play 'The Trumpet Shall Sound', but I suggested that what Ted would really have appreciated would be a brass choir playing a beautiful hymn. This I organised with 8 ex-Heath players, and the result was so warm and memorable that there were many misty eyes among the congegation, and the musicians. I was so proud to do this for Ted. He really was a special person."

Ronnie Scott, tenor saxist in Ted's original line-up. He later left the band to concentrate on the avenues of progressive jazz and formed a number of bands of his own over the years.

Kenny Baker, who was in there at the beginning when Ted formed his first band.

Someone else who regarded Ted as a special person is another who was a founder member of that great organisation — Britain's top trumpet star for many years, **Kenny Baker.**

Born in Withernsea, Yorkshire, Kenny's musical career began playing the cornet in local brass bands, before he eventually moved to London to play in the outfits of Lew Stone, Ambrose, Jack Jackson, Jack Hylton and Geraldo.

During his 5 years with the RAF he was called on to play the trumpet in many forces programmes, and occasionally worked with the Squadronaires — with some of these shows opposite the Glenn Miller band. At the end of the war Kenny was offered the lead trumpet job in the new band that Ted was busily organising, and in 1946 he became a founder member as a featured soloist and arranger.

Kenny stayed with Ted for 5 years before branching out to form a band of his own. "I enjoyed all my time with Ted's band," says Kenny. "It allowed me to write, and I was pleased to have produced 'Bakerloo Non-Stop', Ad-Lib Frolic', 'Dark Eyes, 'First Jump' and 'Filigree'.

The band which Kenny formed, the Baker's Dozen, included pianist Stan Tracey and the late Tubby Hayes, and it was heard regularly on the radio in the Fifties on a weekly late-night show called "Let's Settle For Music". The series lasted throughout the decade.

Also during this time he worked a great deal in the film industry and recorded, on the soundtrack, the trumpet solo which actress Kay Kendall mimed to in the film "Genevieve". He also worked regularly with Robert Farnon and Stanley Black.

Due to his ever-increasing success Kenny was persuaded to work as a solo artist. This he did by touring the country in variety and playing the club scene which, by this time, was starting to get off the ground in a big way. All through the Sixties he was steadily building his reputation as one of the best trumpet players in the world — even though he played very rarely outside the UK.

At the end of the decade he was featured in Benny Goodman's British band, and Kenny's career continued throughout the Seventies with his appearances as the co-leader of the Best of British Jazz touring package, together with the Ted Heath re-creations and the bands led by Don and other former colleagues such as Jack, whose orchestra he joined at the ATV studios, Elstree.

In the early Eighties, and because it would have entailed him uprooting and moving to live in the States, Kenny turned down a unique invitation to take over the leadership of the Harry James band after the latter's death. In this country he could still be seen playing concerts and club engagements and he was heard on television, usually off-camera, playing soundtracks for Alan Plater's popular television series' "The Beiderbecke Affair" and "The Beiderbecke Tapes"

"Ted was excellent to work for and he gave us all a lot of encouragement. Everyone worked so well together. He insisted on punctuality, good appearance and behaviour and, of course, good musicianship; in other words a true professional attitude. Ted was strict — but one needs to be to run a band."

Like his colleague in that original line-up, Stan Roderick, Kenny also missed out on the trips to the States. "I'd left by then," he says, "but I have happy memories of the trip we made to Scandinavia, Denmark and Sweden, because it was just after the war and Sweden was a land of plenty — which made quite an impression.

"I feel very proud to have been a part of this great band, and particularly pleased about the fact that I was one of the first musicians who Ted asked to help him to form a band that was to become so famous."

In every pack there is a joker and today in the Ted Heath band, as in his 18 years previous, that particular character is **Duncan Campbell.**

In fact such a comedian is trumpet ace Duncan that one of the first things he told me about Ted is that his favourite meal was bacon, egg and tinned tomatoes! Now then, you must admit, not a lot of people know that!

But if you've ever had the experience of seeing this extremely lovable personality playing "Tequilla" — through his nose — then you can well imagine what it's like when you are in his company.

It's laughs all the way and anything can happen, and it usually does!

Duncan Campbell

A young Duncan, in his early days with Ted's band, seen enjoying a spot of jamming with bassist Johnny Hawksworth and drummer Ronnie Verrell.

When Duncan joined up with Ted in 1951 he stayed with him until the band broke up prior to Ted's death. For 10 years, without a break, he played in the band's renowned trumpet section which remained intact during the whole of this period, and which also included Bobby Pratt, Bert Ezzard and Eddie Blair.

In November last year Duncan, along with fellow musicians from the Heath Band, Ronnie Chamberlain and Bobby Orr, formed part of Ray McVay's band which backed America's legendary Four Freshmen on a tour of this country.

At their Stockport concert I met up with **Bob Flanigan** and Duncan — both friends from the days when Ted's band backed the Freshmen on its first US tour. Bob, the last remaining member of the original Freshmen, and now a sprightly 63 years young, told me: "The tour with the Heath band in the States was one of the most musical and fun tours I have ever been a part of — in fact, it was the best. And in those days I toured with Stan Kenton and many others in venues all around the world. But, I have to tell you, your Ted Heath was the greatest."

Duncan's best memory was the band's Queen Mary voyage to the States for the first tour, and then performing the Carnegie Hall concert in the company of all the big names. Also, names just as big sitting out there in the audience like Tommy Dorsey, Benny Goodman and Louis Armstrong who had all gathered to hear Ted's band play. For Duncan, personally, it was the most exciting concert that he had ever played in.

"It was fantastic, and the band played beautifully. There are so many memories of those American visits with the band, but one night in New York sticks out in particular when Eddie Blair and myself came across this club. In we went and discovered that marvellous trumpet player Clifford Brown was playing there. We stayed until 4 in the morning," he recalled.

"Another time, on the West coast, on one street next to Sunset Boulevard, there were all these clubs right next to each other. In one we heard Jack Teagarden, in the next was a tenor player called Georgie Hall and then we popped into another club and sat listening to a couple of really great players, Frank Rosolino on trombone and altoist George Mariano.

"But everywhere that Ted took his band it was packed to capacity. I don't ever remember seeing any empty seats for the Ted Heath band in those days, because that was *the* band."

Duncan is just one of literally dozens of Heath fans and musicians who have never failed to mention Ted's signature tune, "Listen To My Music", and like the others it has a special meaning and significance for him.

"To me it is the most magical introduction to any band that has ever been. Maybe it's because I was in that band, but I think it's because it is an original — Ted's own composition. Wherever we went in the world we were always nervous going out on stage. Yet as soon as we started to play that signature tune we knew we couldn't go wrong — and that was the same in Carnegie Hall and all the other great venues.

"Wherever we were, and as soon as we struck up that number, that was it! We just couldn't fail. But that band, it was always a winner. There were no passengers on board in Ted's outfit — certainly not! Everyone played like a man."

Duncan is quick to unreservedly apologise if he inadvertently treads on anyone's toes by virtue of his beliefs about Ted's band, and its place in British big-band history. In short, Duncan thought that the band was ahead of its time.

'With all due respect to the many Ted Heath fans in this country, I must say that the band was more thought of in America and other parts of Europe. Because in this country — although people liked big bands — they were more for the commercial dance bands. As a matter of fact a lot of people used to say, 'Oh, Ted Heath, he's too loud', and they'd hold their ears.

"But when you think of that band, and you think of all the rubbish that's around today, it had only one small microphone out in front, and a couple of little speakers. Today, when a band goes out on the road, there's a mike for every single trumpet, trombone, saxes — the whole bit.

"With one mike we used to play great acoustic sounds, and we could fill the Royal Albert Hall. What a sound that band had! — a big, healthy sound because everybody put 100 per cent through their instruments. I only feel sorry that Ted didn't live a bit longer, for he created a unique and wonderful band. Think of this: every single member of that outfit was a soloist, not just the odd one or two, but everyone. And yet, at the same time, we were still all members of a great musical team — a machine."

To underline what has already been said at various points throughout this book, Duncan went on to add weight to Ted's philosophy regarding his skills as both a personnel officer and an employer.

"Ted always went for the best musicians he could get — not the cheap ones — and every one of them got the same money all the way down the line, and that's why we all played our hearts out for the great man. The trumpet section didn't change for 10 years, and that's why it always sounded so well balanced. The chair that changed frequently was the tenor sax; we had people like Don Rendell, Red Price, Bob Efford — all wonderful players, of course — and then along came Tommy Whittle.

"Those great Sunday shows at the London Palladium were so successful and we always played to a sell-out audience. But they were very nerve-wracking, yet with a fantastic atmosphere. Ted always wanted to give his audiences something new and it meant an all-day rehearsal. He was always thinking of different things for me to sing and play and, like I said, it was very nerve-wracking.

"There were times when I thought that it wasn't going to come off, but as soon as that curtain opened and that signature tune was played it had to come off. And it always did! They were great days; wonderful days working with the great Ted Heath, and even now he is so very sadly missed. It was an era that will never be recaptured."

At the time when **Tommy Whittle** joined up with Ted, with whom he stayed for 5½ years, he was the youngest member of the band, and straight away he was struck by the very strong aura of the man. "Ted was OK to work for and was like a father figure to me. Nevertheless, he had this aura or presence about him. He was not a disciplinarian as such — in other words he didn't rule with an iron rod. But his presence made one feel committed to discipline, not only in the act of doing the job, but outside it as well," recalls Tommy.

"When I was in the band I lived next door to Ted's bass player, Charlie Short. He tended to organise things for me, and this was all right until one day when we had to work at Tottenham Palais with the band. Charlie suggested going by Green Line bus, with the route taking us past the Odeon cinema in Marble Arch. But it just so happened that the Queen was paying a visit to that cinema and, of course, the traffic was jammed. We were late for the gig and Ted went mad. The dreaded words 'the sack' were in the air, and ever since then I still have dreams about being late for an engagement. I understand that other members of the band share the same type of dream.

116

"Being with the Ted Heath band was a continuing highlight because of the tremendous ovations which we used to get with every performance. Ted was one of the greatest bandleaders of all time because he created one of the best big bands of all time, and his music lives on and on.

"One thing that always impressed me was that he never seemed to economise on arrangements. There was always a constant flow of new material, and if it was not to his liking it was ruthlessly discarded. He influenced his arrangers in the same way that he influenced his players — by giving them a free hand, but outlining exactly what he wanted and, most important, always having the final say."

When Tommy Whittle was once late for an engagement with the band, the words 'the sack' hung heavily in the air.

In recalling his days with the Ted Heath band, baritone saxist **Ken Kiddier** (left) has many memories which have proved to be immensely invaluable in compiling this particular chapter. The main one, naturally, was his recalling not only the year, but also the date when he joined Ted's fabulous line-up.

The year was 1955 and the date was January 19 — shortly before the band departed for its tour of Australia and New Zealand. Ken replaced the incumbent baritone chair occupant, the vastly underrated George Hunter, who for reasons of his own did not wish to travel around the world for 6 weeks or so.

And from the time of his occupancy, up until the band broke up, Ken never missed a single gig. In his words (or were they actually Ted's?): "Death was the only excuse — and then only if it was absolutely unavoidable!

"Towards the end we all drifted on our separate ways. There was never an actual finishing date as such, for after Ted became too ill to front the band Kenny Baker did it a few times and so, too, did Ralph Dollimore.

"We were also having to contend with all the 'new' music that was being pushed by concert promoters, agents and the media. Pop groups and skiffle bands were much cheaper than 18-piece orchestras, and I fear that we disappeared, along with a good few others, in a purely financial quagmire."

Ken adds a further embellishment here to Duncan Campbell's early reference to Ted's culinary penchant for bacon (or ham), eggs and tomatoes. He says that it sticks in his mind as an occurrence which repeated itself on almost every occasion when they ate at the various cafes and restaurants which were dotted along their yearly touring programme.

"Ted would invariably order ham and eggs. He reasoned that it was a combination which the questionable hygiene of many kitchens of that era could least affect. This in itself can hardly be described as momentous — until one remembers the egg yolks! These would be kept whole until they, or it, remained the last thing on Ted's plate.

"He would pare away the white with the delicacy of a concentrating brain surgeon, until the final *coup de grace,* which we watched with bated breath as surreptitiously as was conveniently possible. Ted would then slide his fork carefully under the lonely, naked yolk and transfer it, unbroken, into his mouth. This feat completed, to his satisfaction, he would then sit back and finish his tea."

118

It wasn't until a number of years later that Ken discovered the reason behind the fascinating egg-yolks trick. It was after the time of Ted's second attack and he could no longer drive himself to the gigs, that Ken leaned over from the driving seat and asked Henry MacKenzie.

"I distinctly remember Henry's sharp intake of breath as Ted, speaking as one might to a slightly imbecilic child, replied: 'If you can eat the yolk unbroken, then you can't drop any of it down your tie'. He turned his gaze once more to the passing countryside, with a sigh that obviously meant he had added me to his already heavy weight of crosses. I never mentioned it again . . ."

In paying his own personal tribute to Ted, Ken is less than hesitant.

"My first tribute must be to thank, in retrospect, Ted's decision to give me the job in the first instance — without which none of the forgoing would have been possible.

Ken Kiddier

"Also to have been allowed the chance to have played for many years with one of the greatest bands in the world, alongside some of the finest musicians in the world, many of whom, sadly, are no longer with us.

Like so many others Ken Kiddier subscribed to Ted's reputation for being a fair man saying, like myself, that he had yet to hear anyone speak to the contrary. Ted was a very disciplined man himself, and he expected his musicians to be likewise. Although, as Ken explains: "On many occasions we (not him) fell badly by the wayside.

"He paid the best money expecting the best performances in return. There were no contracts except for the singers. He figured, quite rightly, that every musician was after your job, and that this well-intended but omnipresent Sword of Damaclese kept everyone at their peak — which of course it did.

"As an ex-trombone player of considerable stature he understood and forgave the occasional cracked or split note as an occupational hazard, but he would come down heavily on reading mistakes and miscounted rests. These were just carelessness, and he would pointedly ask as to what the problem was."

When incidents of this nature happened, and Ted asked that particular question, he would invariably call the guilty party 'Mate', and Ted's 'mate' was well known to all his men. But it was not your average, friendly term of endearment, for it was spoken with an over-emphasised M and a T which was delivered in such a staccato spit as to make grown men quake. Over a period of time every member of the band was Ted's 'mate'!

Another 'mate' was trumpeter Ronnie Hughes. His inclusion to the fold came about shortly after the band had recorded "Hot Toddy", and most will know that in the middle of the number there is a rather nice and soft jazz-orientated trumpet solo from Ronnie. One night the band were playing the number at a dance, and Ronnie's solo was somewhat different to the one played on the record.

During the interval Ted took Ronnie to one side and pointed this out to him, by saying that "Hot Toddy" was a very popular number and that it looked likely to become a hit record. Above all, Ted insisted that Ronnie's solo 'live' should be consistent with the one on the disc. He also wanted to know the reason why it was different.

Ronnie, truthfully, told Ted that during the recording session he had in fact improvised and made the solo up as he went along. He explained the difference by saying that he could not remember the exact chord sequence, and therefore he had not made any notes. Upon hearing this Ted, in typical 'mate'-like fashion, replied: "Well you'll just have to go out and buy the bloody record, won't you?"

Ken recalled another feature of his boss's particular code of self-discipline, by explaining that no matter how late the band arrived back in London after a performance, Ted would still be at his Albermarle Street office early next morning attending to the business.

"I remember when Jack Parnell left to form his own band," said Ken. "Ted doubted whether he would be able to make a success of it. His actual words, as I remember, were: 'You won't be able to make a go of it, Jack — and I'll tell you why. You can't get up in the morning'. Maybe he was right, for Jack's band was fading after an enthusiastic start and he was rescued by the timely intervention of ATV's "Sunday Night At the London Palladium" shows.

"Jack then got down to the business of legitimate arranging and conducting earning himself, then and now, the reputation of being a most qualified leader of orchestras of all types.

"Ted enjoyed the study of horse-racing form. By that I don't mean he was a gambler as such, apart from an occasional flutter on the classics. It was a hobby, and when he opened his briefcase on the coach or train it wasn't miniature scores of music manuscript which tumbled from its copious depths, it was his collection of form books spreading over 5 or more years.

120

"There was also notebook and finely-honed pencil, for this was his only outlet as far as mistakes were concerned. He would study weather conditions on the race day, (wet, dry, cold, warm) geographical location — uphill, flat or whatever — plus varying distances, jockeys' names, weight, how long the grass was (and when it was last cut) plus all the horses' lineage right back to great, great grandparents.

"He came up with the winner (unbacked) on so many occasions that had he not taken up music I have no doubt that Ted could have been a leading racing tipster."

Like any boss in any office or factory they usually acquire a nickname, either respectful or otherwise. Ted was no exception to this rule because in essence, and by the very nature of his position, he was the boss. And so he was nicknamed.

"We called him the Old Man. Ted accepted that, and I think he liked it," said Ken. "It was meant as a mark of respect and used in the context which one might adopt when referring to a tribal chief. Another nickname, never spoken with a trace of malice and to the best of my knowledge never within Ted's hearing, was the one which was conjured up by Frank Horrox one night at a concert.

"We were all assembled on stage behind the tabs in semi-darkness, waiting for the off, with Ted standing in the wings opposite. Ted was a physically big man with a round-shouldered stoop. His complexion was naturally sallow, which was emphasised by stage make-up, plus his distinctive Charlie Chan moustache.

"A nervous stage manager coughed quietly behind Frank and myself and whispered inquiringly as to whether we could see Ted anywhere. Frank looked at the figure of Ted standing in the wings, turned to the stage manager and, with a completely straight face, said: 'I can't see Ted, but there seems to be a Mongolian thug lurking in the opposite wings'. Mongolian Thug stuck. Ted never knew, but I think he would have laughed."

"I loved and respected the 'old man' for his musical ideals, and I feel proud to have been a part of that band. When we gathered together as many of the old band as could be mustered, for the 21st anniversary broadcast, Ted was not well. Ralph Dollimore took the band through the arrangements, while Ted spent the morning sitting quietly in the control box.

"In the break he nodded me into the seat beside him. During our many hours together in the car Ted always leaned over from the passenger seat and spoke in a confidential manner — even though we were alone. He did exactly that on the broadcast. 'What does it sound like, Ken?' he asked. I answered, truthfully, that the band sounded inspired — a special occasion get-together.

"Ted didn't speak for a long time, then he took off his glasses and pressed his thumb and forefinger into his eyes, like you do when your eyes are very tired. He turned in his seat and smiled the saddest smile I ever saw him do. 'I can't tell, Ken. I can't tell if it's right'.

"We never spoke again but the moment is as clear as yesterday.

"When Ted and his music died I can't help thinking of likening it all to Humpty Dumpty falling from the wall: no matter how well-meaning all the king's men may be, they just can't quite put it all back together again."

The third member of the Heath vocal team of the Fifties, **Dennis Lotis,** explained to me that working for Ted was the best apprenticeship any singer could possibly have had. As with the others Dennis, from the outset, described Ted as a very generous man who, when he learned that the singer had been in this country for 5 months — with his wife and son back home in South Africa — he immediately advanced Dennis the money to pay for their passage to England.

Once the family were reunited they were taken into the bosom of the Heath household, and both Ted and Moira always invited them to parties at their house. Although Dennis admits that Ted was a strict disciplinarian, he told me that he was, nevertheless, pliable enough to see reason if ever Dennis had an argument with him.

Ted, pictured autographing records for his fans at a Croydon store.

"For instance," said Dennis, "when we were in residence at the Savoy Hotel in London, I was sitting in the bandroom one night playing and singing a song at the piano. Ted came over to me and said: 'I don't want you singing those songs'. I replied: 'Why not? You hired me as a ballad singer, and all I'm singing is crap like 'Feet Up, Pat Him on the Bo-Bo'. To which he answered: 'You'll sing what I tell you to sing'. My immediate response was an angry, 'In that case you can stick your job up your a . . .'."

After realising what he'd said Dennis started to think, quick, about what he was going to do next. He now had no job, a wife, a 1½-year-old baby and another child on the way. However, all was not lost because the next day Ted phoned Dennis and asked: "You didn't mean all that rubbish last night, did you?" Dennis was only too eager to agree with Ted, who then said: "Good. In that case I'd like you to get together with Reg Owen and sort out an arrangement for 'So in Love'.

"Ted not only realised that I'd spoken in the heat of the moment, but he also placated me by giving me a great Cole Porter ballad to sing," enthused Dennis.

By virtue of his popularity with his female admirers Dennis continued that on another occasion he was, metaphorically speaking, the rope in a tug of war. "We were playing at a dance at Reading Town Hall when I got up to sing 'I'm In the Mood For Love', and a crowd of girls got hold of my legs and started tugging away at me.

"Ted got hold of me around the waist (I was still trying to sing) but the girls managed to drag me off the stand. They then stripped me of my tie, hankie, shoes and socks. I managed to free myself from them, without the items they had taken from me, and I crawled back to the dressing room. Eventually I got my shoes back — minus the laces."

At another town hall dance, this time in Leeds, Dennis was in dread of being mobbed by a gang of female admirers who were screaming, "We want Dennis. We want Dennis". But his plan of action at the end of his performance, once again brought him into conflict with Ted.

"I made my escape via a dressing room window," recounted Dennis. "Later on, back at the hotel, Ted called me over in an exasperated voice and said: 'Don't you ever do that again! Those are the people who will either make or break you in this business, and so long as they want you it's your duty to respect their wishes'.

"It was advice which to this day I have responded to. I have come to realise how satisfying it is when scores of people come up to me and say, 'Thank you for the pleasure you have given us over the years', or 'My wife and I first met at such and such a dance hall when you were singing with the Ted Heath band.

"It's quite amazing the effect that Ted's band had on people's lives. Although I was with the band for only 4½ years, and have done endless television and radio shows, variety, 2 Royal Command Performances, musicals in the West End, played in Shakespeare plus other dramatic roles and appeared in 9 films, it is my time with the Ted Heath band that folk always talk about."

There probably weren't many people who told Ted where he could stick his job but, after an argument with his boss, Dennis Lotis was one of them!

124

Another extremely notable memory of Ted (albeit that concerning his band) comes from **Derek Boulton** recalling the time when Ted decided to take the band off the road for a time in the late Fifties, in order to give his men a break from the almost constant touring.

Derek recalls: "The band was booked to play sweet-style music, instead of its usual material, at the Savoy Hotel in London. After they'd been there for about a month, the boys called Ted into the bandroom one night saying that they wanted to talk to him. In Ted walked and said: 'Right, gentlemen, what can I do for you?' A spokesman for the band — I forget who it was — said: 'Ted, we're not going to play another f...... waltz!'

"In other words, by doing what he thought was a favour for his band, Ted had created a rod for his own back. The boys proved that they preferred the touring, playing their kind of thing, to just sitting there playing boring waltzes all the time."

When the boys of the band had made their way to bed, Ted still found work to do in his hotel bedroom preparing programmes for radio and concert dates.

Don Lusher

In the final contribution to this chapter — and book — I could think of no better person to give his recollections of his memories with that remarkable man, and band, than the man who so obligingly started this work off in the first place. **Don Lusher.**

"I remember my first visit to Ted's office in Albermarle Street when I had an interview regarding joining the band. I felt then the aura of the man and knew that he was something special," said Don.

"I can recall my first week's work with the band when we topped the bill at the Finsbury Park Empire (8 shows), did a BBC broadcast, a Luxembourg broadcast, 2 Decca recording sessions and a Sunday concert! I could not believe the amount that was in my wage packet that week — it brought a lump to my throat.

"Sometimes, if the band was tired or there was too much fun going on Ted would just look at us and say, 'Come along, play properly — play properly', and everything would simply drop into place. At one point, whilst touring the USA, Ted became quite ill. We did 2 shows in Cinncinatti, one in the afternoon and one in the evening. Ted had to keep going off stage to be sick in a bucket, and then he would come straight back on to make the announcements and look after the band. He would never give in."

126

Like the other contributors to this chapter, Don recalls the band's first concert at Carnegie Hall, in New York.

"At the end of the show we were given a tremendous ovation; I looked across at Ted and saw tears of pride running down his cheeks. He was not a man to show much emotion, but this was all too much for him.

"I remember, too, the time when Ted asked me if I would one day like my own band. I naturally replied that I would. 'Good,' he said, 'I'll finance it'. Several years later he told me that he would have to drop the project. The business was changing and he was finding it harder to get work for his own band let alone a new band for me.

"Ted always liked listening to the playbacks when we were recording. He always asked for it to be played back at a low level so that the sound was not flattering. Some of his comments were: 'I can't hear enough of the tune. I can't feel the beat. That part is too busy. It's all too loud'."

There were other memories for Don like the times at Christmas when the members of the band, and their partners, would meet the Heath family. "The atmosphere was lovely, the food, the drinks and the company were all that you could wish for. Ted and Moira's home on the top of Wimbledon Hill was not only beautiful, but also a real home.

"In the States I can also remember seeing Ted deep in conversation with fellow bandleaders like Woody Herman, Les Brown, Buddy Morrow, Stan Kenton and Count Basie — all gentlemen who loved their bands," said Don. "And I will always recall being at the Statler Hotel in New York seeing and hearing Tommy Dorsey's band. It was magnificent. Ted turned to me and said, 'You will never hear anything better than this, Don'."

There was just one time when life with Ted was not to be cherished by Don, and that was when he went to Ted's office to give in his notice.

Don recalls: "I was not looking forward to it. I had been offered the job with Jack Parnell's ATV Orchestra out at Elstree — a very good job. I wanted to stop touring and just do freelance work. Ted was very angry and tried hard to talk me out of leaving, but I said I must leave.

"During the period of my notice he never spoke to me, and he cut me out of a lot of my features. He was hurt at the thought of anyone wanting to leave his band, which he believed was the best thing in the world. Looking back I can well understand his feelings!

"Of course I missed the band a great deal and eventually Ted called me to do a few things with the band. He was fine to me, and that certainly made me feel better."

Those, then, are the thoughts, feelings and terms of respect, endearment and admiration from some of the many musicians and singers who passed through the ranks of the Ted Heath band, and the man who led what was universally regarded as the greatest swing band in the world. And who would argue with such views? Doubtless, since they gave me their recollections, others will have sprung to mind.

However, one thing is certain: any afterthoughts are bound to be favourable, for it became apparent when writing this book that no one had a single adverse thing to say about the man. Ted Heath was unique — a one-off in the world of big-band swing music, with the main emphasis being on the word "world".

Finally, from my own point of view, I can only repeat the words which I used in that BBC radio interview to sum up this great bandleader and his music: *"There has never been a band so unique, so polished, so professional and so popular as that of Ted Heath's. The sad truth of the matter is that there never will be again, either."*

━━━━━━━━━━━━━━

● There is no doubt that the memory and the music of Ted Heath will never die and if, after reading this book, you wish to keep that memory alive then why not become a member of the Ted Heath Music Appreciation Society? You can do so by contacting Pete Jones, 2 Tempest Road, Egham, Surrey TW20 8HX. Tel: 0784 451292. You, too, will then become an integral part of what was — and always will be — The Greatest Swing Band In The World.

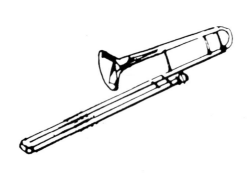